MONEY,
Real Quick

Kenya's Disruptive
Mobile Money Innovation

Tonny K. Omwansa & Nicholas P. Sullivan

Balloonview

Published by Balloon View Ltd, www.balloonview.com

Designed and set by ALS Designs, www.als-designs.co.uk

Printed and bound in Great Britain by
CPI Group (UK) Ltd, Croydon, CR0 4YY

ISBN: 978-1-907798-45-0

Using individual stories, interviews with key players, and research studies as its sources, the authors take you on a journey from the beginnings of M-PESA to its possible, future role as the harbinger of a cashless or "cash light" economy in Kenya.

Guy Stuart, Fellow, Ash Center, Harvard University

****

This incredible story of M-PESA is a very easy read! As a policy maker in the financial sector in Kenya, I recommend it to those interested in how mobile technology can extend financial services to the last mile.

Professor Kinandu Muragu, Executive Director, Kenya School of Monetary Studies

****

With this well-documented, comprehensive and lively book, we can now all go on an "armchair M-PESA safari." It's a gripping tale, written in a straight-forward manner suitable for all audiences.

Ignacio Mas, mobile-money expert

****

This book is full of fresh, new perspectives on the history of M-PESA and, perhaps, more importantly, insights into what's next for M-PESA and mobile money.

Dylan Higgins, CEO, Kopo Kopo

****

What a great read! I am so excited that Kenya now leads the world in a non-traditional area. It's a tremendous story of success with great potential still to be exploited.

David James, CEO, Musoni

****

A brilliant overview of the "killer app" that not only captured the hearts and minds of Kenyans but also showed the world that there is tremendous value in the unbanked segments of the population.

Dr. Olga Morawczynski, manager, AppLab Money Incubator, Grameen Foundation

CONTENTS

INTRODUCTION 7

Chapter 1: THE INNOVATION 17

Chapter 2: THE HUMAN NETWORK 41

Chapter 3: BANKS DISRUPTED 57

Chapter 4: IMPACT AT THE BASE OF THE PYRAMID..............79

Chapter 5: INCHING TOWARDS "FINANCIAL INCLUSION"..... 97

Chapter 6: SWAHILI SILICON VALLEY 117

Chapter 7: CHANGE IS NOT EASY 137

Chapter 8: KENYA ON STAGE 151

Chapter 9: CASH IS THE ENEMY! 171

ACKNOWLEDGEMENTS 189

INTRODUCTION

Changing Lives: Innovation, Disruption and Transformation

"Mobile phone technology has in a few years of its existence demonstrated how financial inclusion can be leapfrogged on a major scale and in a short time span using appropriate technological platforms."

Njuguna Ndung'u, Governor, Central Bank of Kenya

"A world first, M-PESA is indeed a disruptive, leapfrog idea. A continuation of Professor Schumpeter's creative destruction with a Kenyan face."

David Mataen, Columnist, The Daily Nation.

****

Two-and-a-half billion adults in the world don't have bank accounts, but about half of these unbanked have mobile phones. Many of those phones are being used to send, receive and save money. People who first used a phone five or ten years ago and never had a bank account are now transferring money by phone.

In countries where money means cash and cash typically moves by bus or post, the move to mobile is reducing transaction costs, and increasing the velocity and productivity of money. For the banked, mobile money provides superior speed, convenience and safety. For the unbanked, mobile money forms the beginning of a shadow banking system. For everyone, cash is the enemy – expensive to print, hard to store and move. Dematerializing money is good for people rich and poor, businesses, and governments.

Mobile money, e-money, e-float, e-wallets, mobile banking, however you characterize it, is not just a cool app. It's a killer app, the first for mobile phones in the developing world. It's also a disruptive innovation that threatens incumbent businesses and is sparking new business formation and entrepreneurship.

Nowhere is this mobile money phenomenon more prevalent and successful than in Kenya, an East African country of 40 million people. In five years, 19 million Kenyans, more than 70% of the adult population, have signed up for mobile money services. Fifteen million are customers of M-PESA ('M' for Mobile and PESA means money in Swahili), the mobile money service offered by Safaricom, the leading mobile operator in Kenya. It took 115 years for banks to provide their customers with 43 licensed commercial banks, 1045 bank branches and 1,500 ATMs; in roughly five years, Safaricom has provided its customers with more than 30,000 M-PESA agents, where people transform cash into e-money, or e-money into cash. In 2011, $10 billion moved through M-PESA, according to World Bank and Safaricom projections.

It's now far easier to send money person to person in Kenya than in the United States. In fact, one out of every two people in the world who sends money over a mobile phone is a Kenyan. Mobile money is the rare case in which an African country is the global market leader and an exporter of innovation.

If the mobile phone revolution in developing countries was Leapfrog Round 1, as people gobbled up information and communications technology

(ICT), the mobile money revolution is Leapfrog Round 2. Mobile phones were adopted at a faster rate than any technology in history; mobile money, in Kenya at least, is being adopted at a faster rate than mobile phones. If the mobile phone revolution in the South equates to the Industrial Revolution in the West, what is the parallel for the mobile money revolution?

It's too early to say, but Kenya hints at where this is going. Every day, M-PESA transactions in Kenya outnumber Western Union transactions globally. Every day, 60% of all electronic financial transactions in Kenya go through M-PESA, a flow equal to more than 20% of the country's GDP. Those big numbers actually represent a very small slice of the Kenyan money supply, less than 1%. But the massive flow of a small stock of money is statistical proof of the pent-up demand for a more accessible system of payments. M-PESA is a transactional rail that in five years has created a whole new financial ecosystem, much like the iPhone in Western markets.

The classic banking model doesn't map to the needs of the poor. Banks make money from a small number of relatively large transactions; mobile operators make money from a large number of relatively small transactions. The bank model is based on float, accepting deposits and lending them; the mobile operator model is based on usage, the more the better. Prepaid airtime, bought in very small increments, was the precursor and conceptual foundation for mobile money. Once you have minutes (airtime) in your phone, you are storing value, which you can use or send to others.

Kenya has a cash culture, much like many developing countries, with few credit cards. Kenyans generally don't like debt. In a cash culture, cash is both saviour and enemy. If people know you have a lot of cash, you and the cash are at risk. Storing it at home or transporting it is difficult and often dangerous; storing it in a mobile phone is virtually foolproof. If your phone is stolen, the robbers don't have the two PINs (one for the phone, one for M-PESA) to hack at your money.

For small retailers, service providers or merchants that engage in numerous cash transactions during the day, the ability to transfer money to their M-PESA accounts on a regular basis provides peace of mind. The ability to send immediate payments to suppliers by phone makes up for the lack of credit, and that greases supply chains, long calcified by the need for cash.

When M-PESA was first introduced, the early adopters were better educated, higher-income males living in the capital city of Nairobi, which is the business and financial centre of East Africa. They used M-PESA to send money to relatives in rural villages; it was better than taking a two-day bus trip or virtually any other money transfer method. This natural urban-rural remittance pattern gave M-PESA a ready-made market and slogan – "send money by phone" – which was popularized as "send money home." It also forced those on the lower end of the economic spectrum to subscribe to M-PESA and learn how to use it – if only to cash out money sent from the cities. While M-PESA subscribers as a whole are still more upscale and more likely to have bank accounts than the population at large, the profile of M-PESA subscribers has steadily shifted to increasingly reflect the Kenyan demographic in terms of gender, income and geography. Nearly half of those in the lowest income quintile now use M-PESA; nearly half are women. M-PESA is clearly affordable, especially when compared to the opportunity costs of transporting cash by hand. It is also faster than using money transfer companies and more convenient than using the formal banking system.

Even the Kibera slum, on the outskirts of Nairobi, where over 250,000 people live cheek by jowl in highly unsanitary conditions and makeshift housing, is a beehive of M-PESA activity. There are very few bank branches, but M-PESA agents line the dirt streets; people queue up to fill their phones with e-money and/or collect cash. Savings groups, once a high-touch face to face phenomenon, much like micro-lending, have in many cases adopted M-PESA as a means of mobilizing lump sums to lend amongst themselves.

One reason for this seeming incongruity is that M-PESA has unleashed entrepreneurship, and entrepreneurs see demand waiting to be filled. Running an M-PESA agency is one of the better entrepreneurial opportunities in the developing world. With a KShs 20,000 ($250) stake to set up an e-float account, you can register as an agent, set up shop, hire "cash merchants," and prepare for a parade of customers. However, the need to have sufficient float pushes the bar for capital outlay higher. Some agents make more than doctors, lawyers and other professionals, especially "aggregators" that operate multiple agencies and sub-agents (aka cash merchants).

The entrepreneurial spirit that brings M-PESA to the poorest of the poor living in large slums also brings M-PESA to the most remote areas of the country. In distribution, whether it's for high-value, high-tech broadband and services or low-tech products such as malaria nets, the last mile is often the hardest one. You can deliver products to a distribution warehouse or network point, but moving goods from small towns into the hills over rutted or nonexistent roads is a vexing problem.

Coca-Cola has solved this problem better than any company or NGO in the world. Go almost anywhere in the world, to the deepest jungle or the end of the most remote rural road, and you will likely find a Coke. The vaunted Coca-Cola distribution system is considered the benchmark by which others measure their efficiency. Today, many consider that M-PESA is doing a better job of reaching into the furthest corners of Kenya than Coca-Cola itself. [One innovative NGO, ColaLife, leveraging mobile money networks, has even devised a way to deliver medical supplies on Coke trucks (albeit in Malawi, not Kenya), packing oral hydration tablets and other necessities in AirPod containers that fit between the bottles in the crate.]

But Safaricom is no NGO. It has leveraged its dominant market share (about 80%) to build a whole new business and profit centre. Safaricom was the most profitable company in East Africa in 2009, although intense competition on voice-call pricing has hurt profitability and arch-rival Equity Bank is now number one in East Africa in terms of account holders. But M-PESA, which accounts for slightly more than 10% of Safaricom's revenues, but more than 20% of profits, moved more than $10 billion dollars in transactions in 2011. "M-PESA is like oxygen to Kenyans," says Betty Mwangi, General Manager of financial services at Safaricom.

****

This book tells a tale of innovation, disruption, and transformation.

Prepaid phones themselves were a business model innovation. Rather than using the postpaid model so common in developed countries, which requires credit ratings and credit cards, the prepaid model opened up telephony to anyone who could buy or access a phone. With no monthly bills, people can buy and use as many minutes as they can afford, as long as they pay up front.

Mobile money transfer builds on that innovation – and the ability to share minutes (airtime) with others. The agent network piggybacks on the vast network of airtime resellers. Again, mobile money is not so much a technological innovation, although the software used and back-office reconciliation is quite sophisticated. Mobile money is a business model transformation whose success is largely dependent on the strength of its human network, the cash-in/cash-out agents.

More importantly, M-PESA is in many ways an African innovation. While the idea and the technology behind it did germinate in London at Vodafone (a large minority stakeholder in Safaricom), the concept was tested, honed and commercialised in Kenya and has succeeded there like nowhere else. At the same time, the fact that a huge multinational such as Vodafone was able to conceive and implement such an innovation is rather extraordinary. Similarly, for Safaricom, which was and is the market share leader in Kenya, the real breakthrough was to move past its telco paradigm and start thinking like a mobile payments provider.

That innovation has led to disruption, brought on by the clash between two radically different sectors: telecom and banking. Mobile operators have now essentially converted the SIM card into an ATM bank card. Far-flung M-PESA agents are human ATMs. Banks first ignored M-PESA, then tried to persuade the Central Bank of Kenya to shut it down; now, they connect their customers to it and are building their own agent-based networks beyond their branch networks. M-PESA has shown that doing business with the poor can be profitable, and banks are implementing the agent model to increase their customer base.

Finally, this is a tale of transformation. In a country where the vast majority of people don't have a bank account, 90% of M-PESA users say that if the system were to crash it would have a "very negative" effect on their lives. Many have signed up for pensions and insurance for the first time, and are making micropayments by mobile phone. M-PESA appeals to all segments of society – rich and poor, banked and unbanked, housed and unhoused, farmers and pastoralists, CEOs and janitors, street hawkers and shop merchants, small businesses and big businesses.

The transactional platform for mobile money transfers is connecting the unbanked to the financial grid, and reducing transaction costs for every financial actor in society. Businesses run better, entrepreneurship is unleashed (Nairobi is becoming a leading innovation hub in Africa), productivity is increased, bills are paid instantaneously, money is redistributed from urban centres and market towns to rural villages, cash flow is smoothed during disruptions in income, just-in-time financing allows economic opportunism, domestic and international remittances are more regular, and the unbanked are slowly integrated into the formal financial system.

Mobile money's potential to further financial inclusion by expanding banking borders is huge, given the billions of people in a range of countries who have long been cut off from a reliable way to manage and leverage their finances. Since M-PESA started, more than 100 mobile money deployments are underway in other countries (as well as Kenya). Most started in the last two years. None have come close to replicating the success of M-PESA in Kenya. Then again, it took more than 1,000 years for the banking industry as we know it today to take shape – and 30 years for the credit card industry to achieve critical mass.

This book tells the story of Vodafone's business-model innovation and Safaricom's execution to commercialise, along with tales from those who benefit from a new financial ecosystem that moves money faster and easier, and connects people to markets and the larger financial grid. It follows the spread of M-PESA to the larger East African Community and around the world, and shows how similar mobile money systems are being tailored to fit the particular contours of distinct geographies and cultures.

Chapter 1
THE INNOVATION

Parasayip Ole Koyati is a Maasai living in Olooloimuitia village, situated in vast grazing territory on the eastern shores of Lake Victoria, north of Tanzania. Olooloimuitia has no electricity, roads or banks. The only Internet access is via mobile phone.

The Maasai people are famous for their traditional warrior lifestyle, diet of meat, milk and cow's blood, and dramatic beaded jewellery. But they are also one of the most impoverished groups in Africa and subject to frequent food shortages. Cattle are central to the Maasai economy. Rarely killed, cattle are accumulated as a sign of wealth and traded or sold to settle debts.

Parasayip Ole Koyati has a large herd of cattle, sheep, goats and camels. He accumulates animals when there is rainfall and pastures and sells when there is prolonged drought – which dries up water and grass for his herd. He sells to the Kenya Meat Commission or to private slaughterhouses.

Before M-PESA, Parasayip Ole Koyati preferred cash transactions, as banks that were needed to cash cheques and make repayment deposits were too far away. However, due to the risk involved in carrying cash, Parasayip Ole Koyati opened a bank account at a distant bank. In a place where there is no public transport, Parasayip Ole Koyati used to walk almost half a day to reach the bank. He would either deposit a cheque or withdraw his money.

When M-PESA was introduced in Kenya, another enterprising Maasai, Titanet Ole Njapit, opened the first M-PESA agency in Maasai Mara, a township next to Olooloimuitia village. M-PESA allowed borrowers to pay back microloans without travelling to banks. This led to a small revolution, as Parasayip Ole Koyati and other low income herders began using loans to expand their herd; some even delved into grain trading networks that had previously been dominated by a few wealthy businessmen.

For Parasayip Ole Koyati, M-PESA provided a credit and saving facility, as well as a payment system for his cattle. He now prefers payment via M-PESA; he gets his money immediately, and doesn't spend a day walking to the bank and back.

As M-PESA continues to grow, more benefits flow to the Maasai. Initially, very few Maasai had bank accounts. Now, they have embraced M-PESA as their bank. Parasayip Ole Koyati is able to deposit money via M-PESA at Maasai Mara, and later transfer it to his bank account. This is possible through partnership programmes between banks and M-PESA. In this peaceful, pastoral section of Kenya, the unbanked are joining the banked.

****

The banking industry in Kenya is about 115 years old. By 2006, a year before M-PESA launched, the country's 41 commercial banks had developed 400 bank branches, and 600 ATMs to serve 36 million Kenyans. An in-depth survey (FinAccess 2006) that year by Financial Sector Deepening, a Nairobi-based independent Trust established to support the development of inclusive financial markets in Kenya, found that only 18.9% of Kenyans were "banked," 7.5 % had access to "other formal" financial instruments like microfinance institutions, 35.2% accessed "informal" instruments such as savings groups, and about 38.4% were. "financially excluded."

Did the "excluded" have money to move? Did they actually move it? Did they trade using cash? Did they save? Did they pay any bills? Yes, yes, yes, and yes. The financial lives of the poor are complex, with hundreds of hedges every week. In the FinAccess study, those with bank accounts were asked how they felt about banks: 61.5% agreed that they could easily live without a bank account, while 47.1% said that banks took advantage of poor people.

The Central Bank of Kenya was shocked by the report, the first of its kind. The Bank was, in effect, presiding over a moribund banking system that served a thin slice of urban and business elites, while cutting out the majority of its citizens. In huge swaths of the country, you'd have to travel for hours to find a bank branch, and once you got there it might be closed. The cost of branch and teller maintenance meant it just wasn't profitable for banks to maintain branches serving poor customers with minute transactions.

In 2000, a similar critique could have been levied against the telecommunications industry. In its 60+ year history, the monopolistic government owned Kenya Telecom had provided its citizens with a pathetic communications system. There were certainly more phones than banks, but not by much, and they were also confined to urban centres. In 2000, with a mere 309,379 landlines, the phone penetration rate was 2% – meaning that 98% were "unphoned."

By the time of the 2006 FinAccess study, however, the phone penetration rate was about 35%, thanks to 10 million mobile phones. Most were

Safaricom customers; Celtel (later Zain and now Airtel), which was big in 13 other African countries, had a fairly small footprint in Kenya. The daily increase in the phone penetration rate was palpable – phones were selling like hotcakes, along with top-up cards, connecting people to each other and markets like never before.

With minimal infrastructure grids for banks, landline phones and transportation, the exponential rise of mobile phones was the grandest infrastructure development in Kenya since the railroads of the 19th century. And if a small number of banks sent large amounts of money to each other electronically every day, why couldn't a large number of people send very small amounts of money to each other – every minute? It's much cheaper and faster to scale technology than to scale huge telephone transformers and hulking ornate bank branches, both of which require masses of capital, not to mention transformative business models to deal with new markets.

SEND MONEY BY PHONE

"Send money by phone" was the initial and is still the primary value proposition for M-PESA. It was brilliant positioning, as the benefit of texting money to remote rural villages was immediately clear to most Kenyans. *Harambee* and *Sambaza*, Swahili words meaning to "all pull together" and "distribute", are concepts deeply embedded in Kenyan culture. Sending money to relatives by M-PESA saves time (often days) and is much safer than carrying large amounts of cash. Everyone – the *wananchi* ("common people") – wants to send money home.

The product concept is simple: an M-PESA customer can use his or her mobile phone to move money quickly, securely and across great distances, directly to another mobile phone user – person to person (P2P). The customer does not need a bank account, but registers with Safaricom for an M-PESA account. Customers turn cash into e-money at M-PESA agents – there are more than 30,000 spread out across the country, compared to 1,500 ATMs – and then follow simple instructions on their phones to send payment (much like SMS) through their M-PESA accounts. There is no charge to sign up or deposit money, but minimal charges to transfer funds and withdraw cash. M-PESA is simple to understand and use, fast and safe to execute, and extremely convenient. During the 2011 holiday season, Safaricom recorded 285 M-PESA transactions per second, as subscribers sent money to loved ones. When schools open, parents and guardians heavily use M-PESA to send school fees and pocket money.

To register as an M-PESA subscriber, all that's needed is a national identification card (or an equivalent, such as a passport), which every adult has. The subscriber is given a PIN number, similar to a bank PIN. In essence, the cell phone's SIM card functions as a high-powered ATM card. When a customer is withdrawing cash from an agent, he or she must provide the national ID card, enter the agent's identification number and the PIN into the phone. The account is secure – as secure as an ATM card, at least. A deposit requires the ID, PIN and cash.

But that seemingly simple and startlingly efficient system of moving money electronically over great distances resulted from innumerable iterations to synch the value proposition with the business model. When M-PESA was initially conceived, it was a mobile microfinance product, to reduce the inefficiencies of microfinance institutions. The big leap forward came with the realization that M-PESA had much higher value for all kinds of users.

M-PESA is a noteworthy innovation for two reasons. First, the idea that a huge multinational such as Vodafone, the largest mobile operator in the world, could conceive and develop such an extraordinary offshoot to its core business is highly unusual. Second, while most of the conceptual and technological development was done in England, M-PESA was built into a commercial product after more than two years of testing on the ground in Kenya, making it an African innovation that has become a point of pride for a nation re-emerging as an economic engine.

THE SETTING

Kenya is an African country of 40 million people, geographically a little smaller than France. It's bordered by the Indian Ocean on the East, and ringed counter-clockwise by Somalia, Ethiopia, Sudan, Uganda, and Tanzania. Its southwestern corner forms the eastern banks of Lake Victoria, near Mt. Kilimanjaro; from there, the vast Serengeti Plain and Maasai Mara National Reserve (home of the wildebeest and the Big 5 game – lion, elephant, Cape buffalo, rhinoceros and leopard) turns into the pastoral Rift Valley and runs northward toward Lake Turkana, a paradise for pink flamingoes. To the east is majestic Mt. Kenya. The northeastern third of the country is semi-arid, and sparsely populated, with porous borders into Ethiopia and Somalia. The equator runs through the middle of the country.

Kenya's capital of Nairobi has long been the trading and financial capital of the East African Community, which includes Tanzania and Uganda (and recently added Rwanda and Burundi). Mombasa, on the

Indian Ocean, and Kisimu, on Lake Victoria, are the other two big cities, but the country's population is 78% rural.

Kenya is an enterprising country, with a largely agricultural base (tea, coffee, corn, wheat, sugarcane, fruit, vegetables, dairy products, beef, pork, poultry, eggs), but suffers high unemployment (circa 40%) and a 50% poverty rate (average income per capita is about $1600).

From its independence (from the British) in 1963 until 2002, Kenya had two presidents, Jomo Kenyatta and Daniel Moi. President Mwai Kibaki has been in power since, but his re-election in December 2007 brought charges of vote rigging, which led to two months of horrendous tribal violence in early 2008 in which 1,500 died. That led to a five year power sharing agreement with the opposition leader, Raila Amolo Odinga, as the Prime Minister. In 2010, Kenya's parliament adopted a new Constitution, the first since independence, which will eliminate the position of Prime Minister in the next general election (expected in 2013).

Kenya is known to produce great long distance runners, who have broken records over the years. Kenya is also known for great safaris. Now, some people consider Kenya as the world capital of mobile money.

M-PESA was launched shortly before the 2007 election, and the ensuing violence, which closed many banks for long periods of time, made it a preferred means of money transfer, both from cities to villages and from villages to large urban camps of people displaced by the violence. "You know, during the post-election violence it was M-PESA that made sure the IDP (internationally displaced persons) camps had food," says Michael Joseph, who was CEO of Safaricom from 2000 to 2010 and oversaw the development of M-PESA (he is now a non-executive board director and heads mobile money programmes at Vodafone). That alone, of course, does not explain M-PESA's success; but it's hard not to view the end of the violence, the power sharing, the spread of M-PESA and a new constitution as reinforcing and powerful agents of positive change.

THE IDEA

The idea of developing a mobile money product in Kenya dates back to 2003. Nick Hughes, who was then Head of Social Enterprises at Vodafone, which owns 40% of Safaricom (the government owns 35% and private shareholders 25%), had became aware of a promising approach to sustainable development. Just as access to communications facilitates entrepreneurial activity, so does access to finance. This access has the potential to create wealth through bottom-up economic activity, job creation and trade.

Getting cash into the hands of people who can use it is limited on the supply side rather than the demand side. There is no shortage of funds, but it's the ability to move money from the sender to the receiver that is the stumbling block. Since the creation of money, the ability to move it from point A to point B has been a fundamental cornerstone of economic activity. Indeed, since the beginning of M-PESA, a torrent of money has flowed electronically, now equivalent to more than 20% of Kenya's GDP on an annualised basis.

DFID, the British government's esteemed development agency, whose director is part of the U.K. cabinet, had formed a Financial Deepening Challenge Fund targeting East Africa. DFID, in fact, was later (2005) to fund Financial Sector Deepening Kenya (FSD), which wrote the 2007 FinAccess report. Perceiving a large gap in the provision of financial services to the poor, DFID's theory was that while microfinance and informal finance had addressed some of the gap, a substantial expansion of products beyond microcredit was needed to tackle financial inclusion on an adequate scale. DFID envisioned new products for savings, money transfers, leasing and insurance – and the need for a new delivery system beyond bank branches in affluent urban centres.

Today, this approach to development is commonly accepted; then, when microcredit was perceived as a panacea for world poverty, it was forward thinking. So was DFID's principle that engagement with the private sector was crucial to find new business models that would be profitable but also have potential development impact. DFID understood that multinationals could unleash market forces to impact development well before C.K. Prahalad's 2004 book, Finding Fortune at the Bottom of the Pyramid, shone full light on the concept.

Hughes' 2003 proposal to use mobiles to deliver financial services, particularly microfinance loans, was awarded 1 million pounds by DFID. Vodafone would match that in kind with a combination of cash and staff time. Hughes organized a series of open workshops in Nairobi and Dar es Salaam (Tanzania) – inviting banks, microfinance organisations, technology service suppliers, NGOs with an interest in microcredit, and telecom and banking regulators.

This diverse array of stakeholders with often conflicting agendas would appear to have killed any positive outcome. But the concept was to bring together several parties with different competencies to tackle the needs of the unbanked. Hughes and the team then systematically reviewed an ideal partnership mix and settled with a proposed memorandum of understanding between Commercial Bank of Africa, Faulu Kenya (a microfinance institution) and Safaricom/Vodafone.

Network operators bring connectivity and reach through the airtime reseller network; a microfinance institution understands the market need for microloans and other services but is typically not regulated by the Central Bank (unless it takes deposits); and a commercial bank brings the discipline and compliance aspects of storing and managing customers' funds.

With support from U.K. based consultants, business requirements for a mobile money platform were issued through a formal RFP. Early ideas for how the mobile product could work included designing a mobile platform as a module integrated into core banking technology. But this concept looked inflexible and was seemingly expensive to build, so the team turned its attention to a standalone system. Hughes selected a relatively small but innovative company based in the U.K. (then called Scientific Generics, now Sagentia) to design and build the software for M-PESA.

To manage the project on the ground, Hughes engaged Susie Lonie, who had a background in mobile commerce with Vodafone in Europe. She arrived in Nairobi in 2005, for a three month assignment to run a small scale pilot to improve the efficiency of microfinance loan repayments. In the process, Hughes and Lonie realized they were onto something much bigger than simple loan repayments. Two years later, M-PESA launched as a fully fledged mobile payments service. Shortly after launch it was clear that a number of new features were required to allow M-PESA to reach its full potential. Lonie split her time between Nairobi and Dar as Salaam, determining the detailed requirements for the creation of these new features and supporting the launch of M-PESA in Tanzania. In 2009, when M-PESA had signed up more than 6 million subscribers in East Africa, Lonie was transferred by Vodafone to launch M-PESA in South Africa.

THE PILOT

Hughes and Lonie laid down several guiding principles. The product was specifically targeting the unbanked. Whatever was designed, needed to operate without a bank. Therefore, whatever money was in the system would have to be held by the Commercial Bank of Africa on the customers' behalf. That cash would be mirrored in the mobile system as e-money. The e-money had to exactly match the real money, or the new service might have been in the awkward position of illegally creating currency.

The consumer interface would have to run on a basic mobile phone, as smartphones were not abundant in Kenya in 2005, and certainly not available to the unbanked. It was clear that SMS offered the best compromise between usability, security, and cost. Further, menu driven access by SIM Toolkit, standard software on all SIM cards, offered the best potential for a user friendly experience. (Some other mobile money products use USSD, which is not as user friendly as SIM Toolkit, but access to the SIM is only an option for the controlling telecom.)

Retail outlets would act as mobile money retailers, where consumers could deposit cash into or withdraw cash from "e-wallets" on their phones. Safaricom's large established network of roughly 100,000 airtime dealers across the country seemed to be an obvious initial source of agents, although other outlets would quickly sprout.

Before soliciting trial customers, the fledgling service needed a name. A local ad agency suggested M-PESA – "M" for mobile and *pesa*, the Swahili name for money. In Kenya, most people speak two languages and many speak three. Everyone first identifies with their tribal dialect, of which there are more than 40. Everyone also speaks Swahili, the national language and the language of business through much of East Africa. And English is the language of instruction. The further from the capital city of Nairobi you travel, however, the less English. As this service was initially for the unbanked, many of whom are under- or un-educated, all phone menus and SMS responses needed to be dual language. English is more compact than Swahili, which provided some challenges for translators.

The initial microfinance customers were from Nairobi – the downtown business district City Centre, and Mathare, a slum about 20 minutes from town. The pleasant market town of Thika, with broad streets and bustle, a wholesale traders' post for fresh greens and vegetables sent to Europe overnight from Nairobi, was the third location for the pilot.

Recruiting agents – as Safaricom dubbed them – who could turn cash into e-money and vice versa was surprisingly simple. Safaricom identified airtime dealer stores near target areas, and after some explanation most resellers agreed to take on M-PESA.

Safaricom had been so successful so fast, acquiring 5 million customers in five years, that airtime agents figured another Safaricom innovation could not fail.

One small hitch was the lack of potential agents in Mathare, a slum with seemingly little upside for a financial product. But one entrepreneur perceived a gap in the market. She visited the area, fell into conversation with a local petrol station owner, and a few weeks later had built a small shop on his forecourt that became a thriving business in Safaricom airtime, as well as supporting the M-PESA pilot. This was one of the first of what are now over 30,000 agents all across Kenya.

For the pilot, Safaricom opened a trust account with CBA – to receive cash from the agents. The Safaricom finance team issued an equivalent amount of e-money to them in return for that cash, which they used as "e-float" to service deposits and withdrawals. As agents needed more e-float, they would move more cash into the bank.

The pilot commenced in October 2005. Eight agent stores (and soon thereafter, 15) were given phones with an M-PESA menu; nearly 500 Faulu Kenya microfinance clients were enrolled, given phones, and instructed to use M-PESA to repay their loans. Their incentive was a free phone and a few dollars in their M-PESA accounts.

The pilot involved a large number of consumer transactions. In addition to loan repayments, clients could send money person to person (P2P), buy Safaricom airtime and deposit or withdraw from an agent. It was clear that the vast majority of Faulu Kenya members strongly appreciated the convenience and security benefits of using M-PESA for loan repayments – and more. It was also clear to Safaricom and Vodafone that Faulu Kenya's back office system could not handle electronic payments or record keeping; every electronic transaction was manually logged before being entered into the computer.

Watching transactions on internet screens, Hughes and Lonie observed all kinds of innovative uses of M-PESA, such as:

- People repaying other peoples' loans in return for services;

- Payment for trading between businesses;

- Businesses using M-PESA as an overnight safe because banks closed before agent shops (which is still the case);

- People journeying between pilot areas, depositing cash at one end, and withdrawing it a few hours later at the other;

- People sending airtime purchased by M-PESA directly to their relatives in villages;

- Sending money to people outside the pilot population for various reasons.

With signals like this, executives at both Safaricom and Vodafone realized they might be onto something big – something much bigger than repaying microfinance loans. For Safaricom, the big opportunity was to extend its service into a completely new business as a mobile money transfer and payment service, which would add a new revenue stream and increase customer retention. "It potentially was a very sticky product," says Michael

Joseph. As a primarily prepaid provider, customers could theoretically change operators every time they bought new airtime, although they would, of course, have to contend with new phone numbers.

For Vodafone, it was difficult to keep the momentum going and the investment flowing to scale the system. It was becoming clear that M-PESA had promise and might work in several of the many emerging markets where it had operations; in fact, Vodafone has since exported M-PESA to Tanzania, South Africa, Afghanistan and India. M-PESA might also form the basis of a low cost international remittance service. Globally, international remittances are a $400 billion business, fuelled by migrant workers sending money home. Banks, post offices, and Western Union have historically owned the business, charging high transaction fees (30-40%). Many of the busiest remittance trails, such as Germany to Turkey and Europe to India, are in territories where Vodafone has a presence. Vodafone started with a U.K. to Kenya remittance service; it has now moved into 45 countries. Send Money Home – from far, far away.

However, in the early days M-PESA had no natural home inside a large European centric network operator. Recurring corporate re-organisations meant that Hughes continuously had to justify the multi-million dollar spend and dedicated team to run the platform (more than 25 people at its peak) to a new set of executive sponsors. The M-PESA team moved organisational location four times between 2005 and 2009, and on each occasion Hughes had to argue for its continued existence as a strategic new business for the company.

In December 2006, Hughes flew from London to visit Safaricom, where he and Lonie spent 90 minutes with

Michael Joseph reviewing the service and the pilot. By the end, Joseph was committed to a full launch of M-PESA. Joseph had let Lonie run the pilot without interference, but also with few resources. "I was camping in Pauline Vaughan's office," says Lonie. "She was mentoring me, and I was encouraging her to go to Michael and ask if she could join the team." That wish was eventually granted, and Vaughan, who had been in charge of products and services, became the lead manager for and exclusively dedicated to M-PESA. Joseph was quickly becoming a believer.

Safaricom was not quite ready for a nationwide rollout. The product functionality was right, both technically and commercially, to provide a service that could deliver a healthy profit and meet consumer needs. And the service clearly met the mission goals of the donor, DFID, to increase access to finance amongst poor populations in East Africa (although DFID funding had already run out). But significant redesign was needed to make the service suitable for a full national launch – improved processes, security checks, including full external audit and risk reviews, and implementation of AML (anti-money laundering) systems. The pilot also convincingly showed that collaborating with Faulu Kenya, or any other microfinance institution, would be a millstone during a national launch.

The consumer proposition for M-PESA was compelling enough that attracting customers would not be a problem. Of course, that consumer proposition had to be spelled out clearly. "Send Money by Phone" could not be clearer. In Kenya, as in many developing markets, men and younger families migrated to cities to find work and send money home to family members. Kenyans are culturally disposed to caring for members of their larger family. They used various means to do so, ranging from sending heavily disguised parcels by bus or finding a reliable traveller who can transport cash. But both were risky in a country where highway robbery was commonplace.

To support that proposition, Safaricom settled on three features to provide simple functionality: users could convert cash to e-money (and vice versa) at agent stores; send money person to person (P2P); and buy prepaid airtime direct from Safaricom (without going to a top-up shop/ airtime resellers). The overall package was close to the airtime reseller concept, which everyone understood and used daily, and it was culturally aligned with Kenyans' natural remittance patterns.

After a long legal review, the Central Bank of Kenya was persuaded that Safaricom was not acting as a bank (it didn't propose to give interest or generate loans) and thus not subject to onerous bank regulations for deposit taking. To allay concerns about "know your customer" (KYC) identification and branch banking laws, the M-PESA team proposed a customer registration process with national identity cards, and to enforce a transaction limit of KShs 50,000 (about $625) [That has since been raised to 75,000 KShs (about $940).] In addition, the funds held in the M-PESA system were in a trust account held by a new entity, the M-PESA Holding Company, and could not be touched by Safaricom or Vodafone. Interest would accumulate to the M-PESA Holding Company and be given to a foundation managed by Vodafone and Safaricom for the benefit of Kenyans.

"We talked a lot with Jecinta Mwatela, who was acting Governor of the Bank, and got lots of encouragement, but we got the blessing when Njuguna Ndung'u became Governor," says Joseph. "Why did he give his blessing? Because he came from academia and could think outside of the box! He knew that most of Kenya's economy is in the informal sector. The Bank has no sight of, no records for 70% of the economy."

From Joseph's perspective, M-PESA would leverage Safaricom's dominant market position (close to 65% market share at the time) and reduce churn amongst current users. To scale fast, Joseph launched a widespread multi-media advertising campaign; he recruited agents who agreed to set up agencies in three of Kenya's provinces, so that there would be an array of agents well placed to handle two-way transactions. He set up a new business unit within the company dedicated to M-PESA, and made constant training and monitoring a mission. To quickly build out the agent network, he signed deals with Housing Finance (a mortgage financier), Caltex Fuel Stations and Post Bank, turning selected locations into agencies.

Michael Joseph, in 2011, after he had stepped down as CEO, reflected on those early days:

"When we launched in March 2007, I decided that this is going to be big. I don't know what made me decide that it was going to be big, but I decided that it was going to be big and I was going to make it big. I thought that if people have M-PESA, then people will not leave Safaricom. They would emotionally bond to Safaricom. But did I know it was going to be so big? No. I didn't dream it, none of us did, nobody did. I asked my team, in March 2007, 'What is the current business plan?' The current

business plan was that we would have between 300,000 and 350,000 customers by the end of 2007. That was our target. And I said no, 'I have decided it is going to be a million.' And they said it's impossible. And I said no, 'It is going to be possible. If you don't do it I am going to fire you.' My idea was a million customers, because this was so good and so fantastic. Now, that was the drive that was necessary to make M-PESA successful. Once we got a million customers it became viral. Did we know that we were going to go from a million to 15 million today? No, of course not! Had we known, we would have made some other decisions about where the platform should be housed, how the structure of the bank account should look. We would have done lots and lots of things. But nobody knew."

Within a year, M-PESA had well over two million active subscribers, 10 times the expected number; twice what Joseph had pushed for. The initial subscribers were relatively upscale (and banked) male urban dwellers (the basic profile for early adopters of technology around the globe), but they were transmitting more than KShs 100 million (about $1.5 million) a day to their unbanked relatives all over the country. You didn't have to be a subscriber to withdraw funds, but it was much cheaper if you were, so people started signing up in droves. If you didn't have a cell phone, you got your hands on one. If you didn't know how to use it, you learned. There was money in it!

"From the outside, M-PESA looked like a swan gliding along," Lonie says now. "But below the water we were paddling like fury, trying to avoid the weeds." Betty Mwangi, now overseeing M-PESA says: "I think the challenge we have had is education. Just educating people, getting them to turn to the fact that this is a financial service, do not share your PIN, you know because the society at large is not banked. Think about the rural people, like my grandmother, she has never banked. With the economic success of M-PESA it is obviously targeted by fraudsters."

From the start, Safaricom was adding 12,000 new registrations daily, and has pretty much kept up that pace since launch. In 2009, SMEP Microfinance allowed loan repayments via M-PESA, and Grundfos Lifelink allowed micropayments for water. Safaricom added the Pay Bill function, and Kenya Airways and other airlines allowed ticket purchases through M-PESA; Kenya Power and Lighting Company accepted payments from subscribers. The Bulk Payments function allowed employers and others to deliver e-money to large groups, rather than the messy business of delivering cash. At the end of 2009, M-PESA had 8 million subscribers.

In 2010, Equity Bank and Family Bank allowed connections between its accounts and M-PESA, and several more banks (in addition to Commercial Bank of Africa) signed up as Super Agents to provide agents with e-float. By early 2012, more than 600 (a number that is continuously growing) institutions accepted payments via M-PESA's Pay Bill function, and subscribers totalled more than 15 million – nearly 70% of Kenya's adult population. The network of agents had expanded to 30,000, and the mean distance to an agent was down to 3 kilometres, far less in urban locations. Using an ATM to withdraw cash is faster (albeit a bit more expensive) – if you can find one. In September 2010 alone, M-PESA recorded 28 million transactions, moving $841 million. On any given day, KShs 2 billion is transferred.

If the initial idea was to help the unbanked move money from point A to point B, the success has been unequivocal. E-money is flying around the country, over the heads of lions and elephants. There are more daily M-PESA transactions than Western Union transactions globally; 60% of all Kenya's electronic financial transactions are through M-PESA. That represents a mere 2.5% of the value of all transactions, and the accumulated balance of all M-PESA accounts represents just .2% of bank deposits by value. Taken together, these numbers indicate that M-PESA generates millions of very small transactions, with an average size of $20-$30. And it proves just how pent up the demand was for a financial tool for the masses.

At the same time, banks have begun connecting to M-PESA, and even adopted the agent banking model, thanks to new banking laws that give them more flexibility to bank beyond branches (see Chapter 3, "Banks Disrupted"). This extends the M-PESA network ever further. And it lowers bank costs and begins to make small transactions somewhat more attractive, especially as new products are designed for a new customer base.

But the most important aspect of M-PESA is its universal appeal to all segments of society – rich and poor, banked and unbanked, housed and unhoused, farmers and pastoralists, CEOs and janitors, employers and employees, street hawkers and shop merchants, small businesses and big businesses. The uptake of M-PESA has been faster than the uptake of mobile phones themselves! How can that be? The uptake of mobile phones was the fastest adoption of new technology in history!

Even if the poor and unbanked are still struggling for access to formal financial services, the question now is whether or not it matters. Maybe the formal financial sector will never provide what the poor need; maybe they will craft their own quasi-formal, technology-based, shadow banking system. A decade after mobile phones leapfrogged landline phones, mobile money transfer has leapfrogged the banking system. And people are using M-PESA to do much more than just "send money home." They are using it to manage their lives and businesses, and in the process transforming the Kenyan economy.

****

Fawzia is a businesswoman in Wajir in the northeastern part of Kenya, 496km (307 miles) from Nairobi. The climate is semi-arid and hot. Many inhabitants are pastoralists, while a few practise farming along the rivers after the rains. Transportation is a challenge. Roads are poor, and security is wanting. No transport or courier company operates in the area.

To stock her general store, Fawzia had to use a privately owned bus that made only two trips per week to Nairobi, or cargo lorries that passed through the area to and from the capital city of Juba in southern Sudan. The journey was long and slow, with many stops to load and unload cargo.

Since there was no bank in Wajir, Fawzia stored her money under the pillow and used postal services to send it. It took over a week to send a money order from Wajir to Nairobi. If she travelled with the money, she risked being robbed. When she got her stock in Nairobi, she faced another long and dangerous ride back to Wajir.

While in Nairobi, Fawzia stayed with her daughter and her husband.

That was before M-PESA. Now, with M-PESA, Fawzia can send the money in seconds! There are more than 20 M-PESA agents in Wajir. Transport has also improved. Wajir Airport, formerly used just by the military, was opened to public cargo and passenger planes.

Now, Fawzia can "M-PESA" (it's become a verb) money to her daughter, who then purchases goods for her mother's store and delivers them to public service vehicles plying that route or loads them onto a cargo plane. The goods arrive that evening. The overall reduction in transportation costs and time wasted has made a monumental difference to Fawzia's business.

Chapter 2
THE HUMAN NETWORK

It's midday in the dusty streets of Molo, a western town in the Rift Valley province. At the entrance of Molo bus terminal there is a conspicuous shop painted green with white writing. Green, red and white banners hang off the veranda; similar posters adorn the shop's outside walls. Inside sits Paul Machira, 32. Married with a young daughter, he is an employee of Naypart Communications, an M-PESA agency. Before 2008, Paul was a farmer on the outskirts of Molo town. But this area was hard hit by the post-election violence (PEV) in 2007/'08, when warring tribes disputed the Presidential election results. PEV, as many Kenyans call it, was a watershed crisis in modern Kenyan history, and has led to a peaceful political era of power sharing, and the first Constitution written by Kenyans since independence from the United Kingdom in 1963. Paul and his family were evicted from their home; he lost his farming land and two dairy cows, and watched his house being burnt to the ground.

After losing his livelihood, he moved into an Internally Displaced Persons (IDP) camp in Molo town for a few months. Camp life was difficult, lacking basic human amenities. He had no money, and no bank account, not that banks were open due to security concerns. But he had a mobile phone, through which he received money from distant relatives via M-PESA, which he cashed out at a local M-PESA agency.

That agency offered him a job, and a month of training. At Naypart Communications, Machira serves between 60 and 70 customers a day. In addition, he charges phone batteries, replaces SIM cards, and sells Safaricom airtime and mobile phone accessories. Machira now takes home more money than he did as a farmer, and has restored his family's security.

****

Red and green M-PESA logos – painted over tin, flying as flags – festoon Nairobi, Mombasa and Kisumu streets and shops, as well as those of the many small villages in between, and beyond. If banks are dour and stolid buildings with imposing entrances, M-PESA shops are colourful and eye-catching, located near matatu (small bus) stops and residential neighbourhoods, and the doors are often open. Banks are typically open from 9 to 3, Monday to Friday; many M-PESA shops are often open from 7 a.m. to 9 p.m., seven days a week. Despite these clear differences, many M-PESA outlets mimic the bank teller motif – rows of tellers behind windows or iron facades.

Running an M-PESA agency – or working in one as a cash merchant – is one of the popular entrepreneurial and income opportunities in Kenya today, and attracts people from all walks of life. There is Machira, the former farmer, and Mwai, an economist who started an M-PESA business to supplement his earnings. His Update Agencies also offer photocopying, lamination, sales of phones and SIM cards. There is Susan, who quit a job as a chemist to start Embcomm Network in the Mukuru-kwa-Njenga slum outside Nairobi, and Monare, who quit working in a supermarket and now owns an M-PESA outlet. There is Carol, a 40-ish mother of three school children in the northern town of Kasarani who was a former hair dresser until back pains forced her out of business, whose husband took a loan from a local cooperative to help Carol start her M-PESA outlet. And there is Alice, a high school student who performed well enough on her comprehensive exams to earn a spot at university, but whose parents could not afford the tuition. She is now working at an M-PESA agency earning a salary and commissions while attending secretarial school in the evening.

M-PESA cash merchants are everywhere, packed side by side in cities, in petrol stations and supermarkets, along major roadways, tucked in corners of fast-food outlets, lined along streets in market towns and remote villages. M-PESA merchants earn on average $5 a day, a decent take. Owners of agencies make far more. And aggregators, who own or manage multiple agencies, can make $1,000 or $2,000 a month, more than the average annual per capita GDP.

An M-PESA agency is the nuts and bolts and heart and soul of the M-PESA business operation. The cash merchant is the connection between the ethereal word of e-float and the real world of cash, between the back office electronic recording of billions of transactions and the man on the street, between the urban elites and the rural poor. M-PESA cash merchants turn cash into e-float, and e-float into cash. They form the human network that creates real value for the electronic network. Even as e-money slowly supplants paper money, cash is still king – and mobile phones, for all their magic, cannot dispense cash like ATMs, like live cash merchants.

This minor problem, that cash is king, does little to solve the big problem, that cash is the enemy. The M-PESA mobile network is, in fact, less a true mobile channel for e-money than a new store channel to distribute cash outside the banking system. Nonetheless, this transitional phase gives a glimpse of the possibility of truly dematerializing money into electrons.

"The key to making this thing successful was not the technology per se, it was more the management of it, how would you get this to work," former CEO Joseph says today. "And the key to that was the agent network – the people who would be doing cash in and cash out."

THE NETWORK

A mobile money service depends on a broad, deep, efficient, and trustworthy network of merchants. Just as a phone or computer is of little value without other phones or computers to connect with, an M-PESA merchant in, say, Nairobi, is of little value without a host of other merchants on the sending or receiving end of the two-way transaction. If a business manager in Nairobi sends money via M-PESA to his grandmother in a distant village, what good is it if she can't readily cash out at a nearby merchant?

"Developing a new distribution network that was not part of our traditional airtime reseller network and getting all the legalities straightened out was difficult," says Joseph. "We needed to get to 5,000 agents quickly, because this is like the chicken and the egg. If we don't have the agents, the customers won't sign up; if we don't have the customers, the agents won't make money." In the early days, an M-PESA agent had to agree to open a shop in three different provinces, to insure that the network would spread throughout the country.

As important as a well-distributed network is the speed with which it scales. Mobile money networks need to scale fast, otherwise subscribers won't be able to transact with others and will lose interest, and agents won't be incentivised to sign up (and they won't get the necessary transactions to become profitable). If the system does not provide ample functionality early on, it will either languish or die. In fact, this has been the norm around the world, with M-PESA the exception that sets the bar for execution.

Since launching M-PESA in 2007, Safaricom has made the recruiting and training of agents a top priority. Early on, Safaricom outsourced the challenge of identifying and signing up agents to Top Image (and later to other agent network managers). After an initial two week training programme, a Top Image rep visits agencies twice a month, to field questions, monitor traffic, and ensure that the merchants are properly recording every transaction in a handwritten logbook. This acts as a backup to the electronic record that is automatically made of every transaction, and, more importantly, coupled with a paper receipt, gives the customer confidence that he can trace his money. Multiply 30,000 merchants by 25 visits a year (each Top Image rep is responsible for about 2,000 merchants), and that's about 750,000 face-to-face interactions between Safaricom and its merchants a year. That's just a top level indicator of how much it takes to build a successful network.

As business increased rapidly, the average number of subscribers per cash merchant did so as well, shooting up at one point from 700 subscribers per merchant in the beginning, to more than 1,200. That ratio vastly increased the number of transactions per merchant, which increased their commissions, but led to complaints from both customers and merchants, who were overwhelmed and unable to fully satisfy their customers' demands for cash or e-money.

Typically, urban regions were selling e-float, and rural agencies were exchanging e-money for cash. In both cases, agents make multiple trips a day to a bank to rebalance their accounts. Balancing cash and e-float is tricky, a never ending process moving cash between banks and agency kiosks and shops.

By 2010, the number of active subscribers per merchant averaged about 600. That reduced the number of transactions per merchant, which, of course, is as dangerous for Safaricom and agencies as too much traffic, as it undercuts the basic business proposition.

Initially targeting airtime resellers, who had built a clientele in high-traffic locations, Safaricom and Top Image then fanned out to recruit petrol stations and supermarkets and other high-traffic distribution points as agencies. The virtue of this strategy was that they weren't dependent on M-PESA for profits but could treat it as just another hot item to sell. Soon enough, as these agencies looked to expand with employees (cash merchants), Top Image focused on aggregators who managed multiple agencies. The virtue of this model is that Safaricom sells e-float to a relatively small subset of its 30,000+ strong network, and those aggregators and agencies in turn distribute e-float to their subagencies and merchants, respectively.

THE AGENCY BUSINESS

An M-PESA agent acts on his or her own account, getting no money from Safaricom, but does sign a contract with Safaricom promising exclusivity, which means that no other mobile money operator or bank can do business with that agency premise. (This, as we'll see in the next chapter, has been the cause of some tension with banks that are looking to build their own networks of bank agents.) While Safaricom does not invest in its agencies, it agreed with the Kenya Commercial Bank (KCB) to provide collateral backing for loans to agencies at favourable rates. KCB has also agreed to set up overdraft protection for agents' working capital, to be delivered through M-PESA.

An agency's central functions are to maintain office space, develop signage and marketing, hire employees (using some combination of salary and commissions), and rebalance cash and e-float so that merchants always have what they need to satisfy customer demand. PEP Intermedius, for example, located in Kisumu on the shores of Lake Victoria and founded in 2004 as a microcredit organisation, began operating as an aggregator when M-PESA launched in 2007. It now manages 150 outlets, eight of which are fully owned by partners Frederik Eijkman and Paul Otieno, with the remainder being franchise operations, for which PEP provides startup capital and liquidity management. PEP's first agency was number 999 (out of 30,000 and counting), which is worn like a badge of honour, much as early Microsoft or Google employees tout their low employee numbers.

Agents are not truly agents, in the sense that they do not represent Safaricom, the way, say, an insurance agent represents an insurance company. "Agents" merely provide a value-added service – converting hard currency to e-money and back. The value they add is trust, especially important given that many of their customers have never used banks before. Many who have never used banks clearly feel more comfortable conducting a financial transaction in a petrol station than a bank; and they feel freer discussing finance with M-PESA merchants than with bankers, hidden behind glass and iron grills. In a large survey of M-PESA subscribers by professors Tavneet Suri (MIT) and William Jack (Georgetown), 95% said they trusted Agents.

The only risk to the customer is that the merchant could take their money and run, or otherwise defraud them of it, but that is a low level risk in any buyer-seller transaction. Further, there is no incentive for a merchant to defraud his or her customers, because the merchant would almost instantly be out of business. Customers can call Safaricom's customer service number (234), where Safaricom has a record of all transactions (of the roughly 300 Safaricom employees dedicated to M-PESA, the vast majority work at the call centre, according to Betty Mwangi). There is, recent events indicate, more danger that scam artists will defraud merchants (who have more money on their phones than their customers) by posing as authorities, than merchants will defraud customers.

Building a nationwide network of trusted agents who are all independent operators requires a complex balancing act that never quite reaches a steady-state equilibrium. There will always be urban agents who can't hold enough e-float to satisfy their customers' demand for e-money, and rural agents who can't keep enough cash in the till to satisfy customers, and thugs who target those who do. But it is a system that fills a void millions of Kenyans have suffered for a century, and its benefits far outweigh any risks, perceived or real. Quite simply, M-PESA is like a bank that provides liquidity and ubiquity.

AGENT INCENTIVES

Selling airtime is a big business all over Africa, and has been for a decade, as the phone penetration rates have increased from less than 10% in many countries to more than 50% (Kenya is over 75%). It's not a difficult business to enter, requiring little capital, and not complex to operate. The customer hands you money, and you hand over a scratch card. The commissions are good (3-5%), and customer demand is incessant and ever accelerating.

The upfront capital requirements for M-PESA are much higher (a minimum of $250 up front, and an average daily balance of $1,250), the margins are lower and a large segment of your customer base needs a lot of handholding. In addition, M-PESA subscribers can buy airtime using M-PESA, so you will lose much of that business; the World Bank's Consultative Group to Assist the Poor estimates that Safaricom now sells close to 20% of its airtime via M-PESA (for which it earned an extra $8 million in lower commissions per month in 2010). To top it off, the volume of cash that goes through a busy shop on any given day can easily top $2-$3,000, so security measures are mandatory.

In the Philippines, where the mobile money concept was pioneered (see Chapter 8), the huge discrepancy between airtime commissions (12%) and mobile money commissions (1%) is a big reason why mobile money has not permeated society as deeply and broadly as it has in Kenya, despite the fact that Smart Communications and Globe Telecom have been offering mobile money services since 2003.

To encourage aggressive marketing by Agents and prime the business with new subscribers, Safaricom pays $1 for each new subscriber – 80 cents to the Agent and 20 cents to the network manager/trainer. For cash deposits, Safaricom pays 11 cents to the cash merchant and three cents to the Agent; for cash-outs, Safaricom pays 17 cents and four cents, respectively. Given that person to person transfers represent 80% of M-PESA's revenues, and that there is a close correlation between a transfer and a deposit and withdrawal, the agency business is riding a wave.

Average gross daily revenue for an agent is about $16, compared to about $4 for an airtime reseller, according to CGAP. M-PESA agents incur much higher daily costs, roughly $11 to $2, the bulk of which is liquidity management and taxes (a 21% withdrawal by the government). The cost of liquidity management is a function of transportation from the shop to a bank, often with security factored in, plus the opportunity cost of tying up so much capital (about $1,250) every day. Nonetheless, CGAP calculates that merchant employees triple the daily profit of airtime resellers, and make somewhere between $4 and $5 a day. Agencies and aggregators, as noted earlier, can make thousands of dollars a month.

As long as people cash in and cash out on a regular basis, the agency incentives are aligned with their interests. Today, it's possible in many places to buy goods at the market with M-PESA rather than cash, but the transaction fees (Kshs 30) to send on small purchases make it better to pay with cash. It's reasonable to expect that as Kenyans become more comfortable with e-money, they will just store and send, and only occasionally cash out e-money holdings (see Chapter 9, "Cash is the Enemy!"). And on person to person transfers, Safaricom alone takes a cut. At that point, Safaricom may have to revisit the incentive structure for agencies to maintain the business proposition.

THE LIQUIDITY TIGHTROPE

As an employee, full- or part-time, the average merchant may make $5 a day, but there is no such thing as an average agent. The more urban the location, the more transactions recorded, but the higher the costs. The challenge is to maintain a high balance of e-float to stock the needs of remittance senders. The more rural the location, the fewer the transactions recorded, and the need to maintain large supplies of cash, a problem exacerbated by the thin density of bank branches that qualify as Super Agents.

The M-PESA agency is buying e-float from a Super Agent and selling it as he or she would sell any other commodity item – except that the commodity is e-money. Imagine a shopkeeper with a large sack of rice, a mental exercise Ignacio Mas used to employ when he was a deputy director at the Bill & Melinda Gates Foundation (he is now an independent mobile money consultant). As customers come into the shop and exchange cash for rice, the merchant's stock of rice declines and his stock of cash increases. When the rice is nearly gone, he must take the cash to buy more rice, thus increasing his stock of rice and depleting his stock of cash. Similarly, as the cash merchant's stock of e-float diminishes, the stock of cash increases. At a certain point, the cash merchant needs more e-float, and takes his cash to the bank to replenish his "store" – or, in the M-PESA nomenclature, "rebalance" to ensure an adequate supply of cash and e-float.

The main obstacles to rebalancing are time and money, both a function of how far the shop is from a Super Agent. Security, of course, is also a factor, as the agent is either carrying a large sum of cash to or from the bank on a well-travelled path, as rebalancing occurs at least once a day, often more. And, as the owner either leaves the shop with employees guarding the till, or sends an employee to the Super Agent with a lump sum, petty larceny is always a possibility.

In urban locations, where there are multiple super agents, these hurdles are easier to surmount; in rural locations, rebalancing can be a daylong merry-go-round. Consider, as an example, Gaudencia, a 45-year old widow and mother of three who owns three stores near Kisumu in Western Kenya. She is semi-literate, speaks no English, and previously sold chickens in the Kisumu market. Her stores are franchised by PEP Intermedius, the Aggregator who helps manage her float, in exchange for 20% of her revenues. One of her stores is near the market, the other two about a half hour bus trip outside town.

Each morning, Gaudencia first visits the PEP office to exchange cash for e-money and vice versa, then visits each store once, finishing around 2, at which point she returns to the busiest store a second time. On Tuesdays, market day, she makes three return bus trips to this store! Gaudencia spends $5 a day in bus fare, and on each leg of her travels is likely to be carrying KShs 80,000 ($1,000). The upside for this enterprising Agent, whose son and daughter each manage one of her stores, is that she often nets $1,000 a month.

PEP Intermedius moves about KShs 3 million a day, in chunks of KShs 100,000, and has roughly 50 employees, as it builds a nationwide network of agencies for M-PESA, as well as banks such as Equity Bank and Kenya Commercial Bank. PEP, in fact, was one of the first aggregators to sever its exclusivity contract with Safaricom, after signing an exclusive contract with Kenya's dominant supermarket chain,

Nakumart, which allows it to offer cash in/cash out services to multiple mobile money players.

MATURING BUSINESS

The agency business is a good one – for Aggregators, Agents, and cash merchants. But it has grown so fast that it is becoming somewhat mature with fewer opportunities for easy profits. "We still get over 500 applications for agents a day," says Betty Mwangi, of Safaricom. "But we have to turn many down because many areas are saturated, and we don't want more agents in those areas."

M-PESA cash merchants number over 30,000 alone, and YuCash, Bharti Airtel and Orange Money have all entered the fray, signing up their own agents. In addition, commercial banks have finally decided to expand their borders beyond branches by hiring agents. But that was only after they tried, and failed, to shut down M-PESA. By 2012, there were more than 40,000 cash merchants in Kenya!

While many agencies have been side businesses connected to other retail operations, such as petrol stations, fast food outlets and airtime resellers, a significant majority have been standalone agencies. As markets become more saturated with cash merchants, the number of standalone agencies is likely to decline. A lot depends on how use of mobile money evolves. If it remains a strict deposit, send and cash out business, that's good for agencies; if the so-called e-money loop gets longer and people are not cashing out, agencies will see their commissions decline.

****

Risper Nyang'au is a trained teacher, married with four children. She has a part-time job as a university tutorial fellow at one of the universities in Nairobi. To supplement her income she has always invested in small businesses, which have enabled her to employ one or two relatives at one time or another. For about 10 years, she ran different businesses, including a bookshop, salons, a cybercafé and a motel.

In 2007, she heard of people running M-PESA shops. Being enterprising, she figured that it was a good business to venture into. She inquired and made a trip to Safaricom for more details. A day later, she was signed up as an agent.

In January 2008, Risper had three agencies, spread out in three provinces [initially, agencies were required to open in three provinces]. One was in Rongai, one in Nairobi and another in Machakos. In the first month, she had made a net income of KShs 80,000 ($1,000). Her shop in Rongai generated KShs 37,000 ($462). She had never made so much in a first month of business, let alone a profit.

The agency business transformed her life. As an early entrant, she benefitted when Safaricom introduced an Aggregator model, where an agent can sign up sub-agents owned by other people but are managed by the Aggregator. Risper now manages 52 shops, spread all over the country; she owns 14, while the others are sub-agents. On average, Risper makes KShs 15,000 ($187) per shop she owns and 20% of the income from the sub-agents.

With the income, Risper is now building a primary school on the outskirts of Nairobi and is entirely able to meet her family needs.

Risper is always on her phone, coordinating float related issues, talking to business partners, interacting with M-PESA cash merchants as well as

Safaricom M-PESA staff. She also has to ensure that cash merchants are well trained and know how to handle different situations. With such a load, Risper had to quit her day job as a primary school teacher.

Despite her success, Risper is unsure if she should expand her business any more. "It's getting saturated and competitive, opening a new shop means more work and the average income is getting lower," says Risper. "I am unsure if I will be making more money." Risper is now exploring partnership with banks to offer agent-banking services or be a cash merchant.

Chapter 3
BANKS DISRUPTED

The name Kiandutu means "a place with jiggers," and the living conditions reflect that difficult environment. A majority of residents have no nearby access to clean running water. The water in the closest river many kilometres away is severely contaminated with human and animal waste. In search of money, people indulge in immoral commercial activities, such as drug abuse, alcoholism and commercial sex.

Julius Juma is a boda-boda (motorcycle) operator by day and a security guard by night at Broadway High School. He has lived in Kiandutu for more than 12 years, 11 of which he has worked at the school as a guard. The 32 year old has a set of triplets – all girls. His wife of nine years is a vegetable vendor outside their residential single room house. He makes at least KShs 200 per day and saves KShs100 per day on his phone when the situation allows. His wife caters for the family's meals while he takes care of the rent, clothing and health needs. Their house rent amounts to KShs 500 per month. The single room doesn't have water and electricity. They purchase six 20 litre mtungi (jug) of water at KShs 2 each. They budget another KShs 20 to take a shower and KShs 5 per visit for the toilet.

Juma lacks a secure place to save his money. He once tried to open a bank account but claims that money was always deducted without any explanations. He was also required to contribute KShs 300 as registration fees and maintain a minimum balance of KShs 500. Were it not for the free T-shirts

*that were being offered upon opening an account,
Juma admits that he would not have opened the
account as it was an impromptu decision.*

*When he was younger, Juma saved his money under
his tattered mattress. Rats devoured bits of some
notes, which nearly drove him mad. Depositing
money in his M-PESA account has helped him get
"discipline". Before, he would pass by the local bar
and sometimes spend his entire earnings on cheap
liquor.*

*M-PESA has solved many problems for Juma, and,
he says, for the "common man." Juma is grateful
that Safaricom charges neither registration fees to
its subscribers nor maintenance fees. After a hard
day at work, he visits an M-PESA agent and makes
his deposit. He is cautious not to deposit money
with the same agent each time, out of fear that
someone may follow his pattern and waylay him
before he makes the deposit. He says that not once
has M-PESA swallowed an ATM card like ATMs do. He
also points out that the queues in the agents' stalls
are shorter than queues in banks. "M-PESA is giving
people a chance to live life the way they want to,"
says Julius. "I can send money all over Kenya while in
my bed, buy airtime from the comfort of my bicycle
and even pay for my drinks."*

****

In December 2008, as the fledgling M-PESA reached
5 million subscribers – more customers than all 43
banks combined – Kenya's then Acting Finance
Minister, Mr. John Michuki, asked the Central Bank to
audit M-PESA. He said he was not sure M-PESA would
"end up well," hinting at vulnerability to money
launderers and pyramid schemes. He asked the

Central Bank to study the "scheme" and pronounce policy to "safeguard depositors." "We want to protect *wananchi* [citizens] from the sharks who want to make money from the misfortune of others."

Gerald Nyaoma, the Central Banker responsible for oversight of M-PESA, and who had been part of the initial Bank audit before launch, had seen this day of reckoning coming. M-PESA had grown so big, so fast. At the same time, it was not clear which government agency really had jurisdiction over M-PESA: the Central Bank of Kenya, or the Communications Commission of Kenya (CCK), which oversees telecoms. The CCK, to date, had identified M-PESA as a value-added telecom service, but deferred to the Central Bank on finance issues.

Money laundering and pyramid schemes, of course, are very unpopular amongst Kenyans. But few Kenyan observers felt the Minister was really worried about money laundering or pyramid schemes. They felt he was worried about the power of M-PESA and what its meteoric success meant long term for the banking industry. Was the minister trying to shut down M-PESA? Or did he have valid concerns about this new mobile money transfer service whose scale might create sudden and irresolvable problems?

Whether M-PESA was a real threat, or a mere gnat on an elephant's back, was unclear. M-PESA was so new, it wasn't clear its good fortune would continue. But it was clear that most Kenyans saw more value in M-PESA than in commercial banks. As in most developing countries, nearly 80% of Kenyans lived in rural communities and had limited access to basic infrastructure. The poor could not access bank accounts because bank branches and ATMs were remote; even if they could – and produce the documentation required for proof of person and address as required by KYC regulations – the cost of opening and maintaining an account was prohibitive. Banking was generally perceived to be for the rich, educated, urban dwellers living near bank branches.

THE BANKERS' PERSPECTIVE

The bankers' main argument was that M-PESA was not proportionately regulated, thus had an unfair competitive advantage – and it was putting the financial system at risk. The Central Bank had created some loose guidelines for mobile money transfers, but certainly no clear regulatory and legal framework. M-PESA, for example, was free to skirt onerous "know your customer" regulations, which made it much easier to sign up subscribers with marginal background checks. Cash merchants weren't even employees of Safaricom, and were total wildcards! And where did the agents get their e-float? From the banks! For that matter, why was Safaricom allowed to have agents in the first place? Banks couldn't use agents.

Adherence to banking regulations certainly drove bank transaction costs up, which is why it was often too expensive to serve the poor, whose low volume of deposits and transactions couldn't cover the cost of building brick and mortar castles with full-time employees. Another secondary impact on banks was that as more money flowed from the cities to the rural villages, banks were under the strain of supplying liquidity, moving cash to meet the demands of agents who were flush with e-float. The banks were absorbing costs to help M-PESA run smoothly! The bankers essentially accused the Central Bank of operating with a double standard

– of giving Safaricom a free ride to undercut their long-established business. As one banker said: "The Central Bank has rocketed M-PESA to the front of the world stage."

Some of these sentiments were driven by the idea that Safaricom was essentially operating as a monopoly, with its 80% plus market share, and controlled the mobile channel. If a bank wanted to create a product and distribute it through the mobile network – as Equity had done with Eazzy 24/7 SMS Banking – Safaricom would charge fees that made the product uncompetitive. The banks were giving and giving, and M-PESA was taking – it was a one-way street.

That was the business argument. The argument on risk said that customers' money might fall victim to money laundering and pyramid schemes, not to mention potential fraud by agents. By now, the Kenya Bankers' Association, representing the 43 banks, had engaged. The bankers claimed that Safaricom had no mechanism to compensate customers in case of loss. As for risk to the banking system, well, it didn't appear that it would "end up well," an ominous warning. A year after horrendous political violence that brought the country to an economic standstill, Kenya could ill afford a collapse of the financial system.

As long as Safaricom was playing around with microfinance institutions on the margins of the banking system, fine. But when what was fast becoming the largest company in Kenya was running the table – for the second time in a decade – how could there not be more stringent fiduciary oversight? Bankers created the impression that M-PESA was a disaster waiting to happen. It was a gamble with people's money and the government was not being proactive in protecting the public interest. If the Central Bank didn't immediately respond to the minister's request for an audit, the government needed to intervene.

SAFARICOM'S PERSPECTIVE

Listening to Michael Joseph, CEO at Safaricom, you would have thought the commercial banks were reading from a totally different script. And they were – based on the fundamental difference between the way banks and telecoms operate. Banks are conservative businesses whose model is predicated on a relatively small number of high-margin transactions. Mobile network operators (MNOs), by contrast, are young and entrepreneurial, and generate profits from a high volume of small transactions. MNOs can scale fast, banks can't. MNOs can reach their clients in seconds, banks can't; MNOs cater to everyone; banks cater to the well heeled. True, Equity Bank, Family Bank and K-REP had developed products for the common man; but they couldn't compete on the distribution side. The discord between these two operating philosophies accounts for the ongoing battle between the banks and Safaricom.

"Some of the banks are saying we are in competition, but I don't think M-PESA is a threat to the banking industry," said Joseph, responding to the Finance Minister via an interview in *The Daily Nation*, one of Kenya's leading newspapers. "What we are doing is filling a gap that the banks have left out. We welcome the audit by the Central Bank since it will verify the concerns and satisfy the regulator that we have put safeguards in place and the risks are minimal." Safaricom's real competitor, Joseph said, were money transfer services like Western Union and PostaPay.

Safaricom contended, rightly, that the Central Bank's legal counsel had already determined, prelaunch, that Safaricom was not acting as a bank. An operational risk audit had also been conducted, to ensure that electronic records were maintained daily and readily available at all times. Finally, because Safaricom backed all e-float by putting cash into a trust account, and could not touch that cash or take any interest from it, there was no risk to the banking system.

Zain [now Bharti Airtel], the country's second largest mobile network operator, jumped into the fray, claiming that Safaricom was given an unfair preference by the Central Bank due to its large market share. Zain had launched a competing money transfer service, Sokotele, in 2007, but it died quickly. A few months prior to the Minister's demand for an M-PESA audit, in October 2008, Zain had applied to the Central Bank for permission to launch a new money transfer service called Zap!, which would be linked to a commercial bank and rolled out across Africa through Zain's 14 subsidiaries. The Central Bank had not yet given Zain clearance to proceed. Along with the banks, Zain had started to express its displeasure about what appeared to them as the Central Bank's double standard.

CENTRAL BANK'S DECISION

The pressure was now squarely on the Central Bank team to exhibit that they had managed the launch approval and uptake within the parameters of the law and public interest.

Prior to the launch, the Central Bank team had done extensive due diligence, something that was not well known to many of the complainants. The Central Bank's legal counsel had provided a legal opinion that M-PESA was not engaged in banking activities. Any cash exchanged for e-money was the property of the customer, not of Safaricom. The customer's cash is not lent, as banks typically deploy deposits, but stored safely in a trust account. And Safaricom paid no interest on customer money, again confirming that the money was not a deposit. When customers wanted their money, they went to an agent and cashed out.

The Central Bank had also engaged Consult Hyperion, an IT consultancy firm, to conduct an operational risk audit, according to a case study by the Alliance for Financial Inclusion, an international group of Central Bankers and financial regulators. Consult Hyperion tested the end to end encryption of the SIM card functionality, which held all of the confidential customer data; reviewed the use of hardware security modules at the M-PESA servers; and ensured that all business processes had embedded security procedures, including live backup. The consultants also checked to ensure that all of the M-PESA systems allowed for comprehensive reporting and management so every transaction could be monitored, individually and en masse.

Because Safaricom was not a bank, it was not technically under the jurisdiction of the Central Bank. However, the Banking Act did give the Bank the general authority to formulate and implement such "policies as best promote the establishment, regulation and supervision of efficient and effective payment, clearing and settlement systems."

Also unknown to the commercial bankers, the Central Bank had commissioned another FinAccess survey by Financial Sector Deepening in October, 2008, but had not yet publicised the results (Fin Access 2009). More than 80% of M-PESA users were satisfied with the system, and 21% said they used M-PESA to store money. Some had minor complaints of fraud, agents running out of cash, or glitches with the mobile network, but nothing serious – certainly nothing threatening to the financial system, which is the Central Bank's main purview. Taken as a bookend to the 2006 FinAccess survey, which pointed to gross financial exclusion, the Bank felt these recent results showed that M-PESA was moving the needle in a positive direction.

Per its initial letter of "no objection" to M-PESA, the Bank had asked Safaricom to track monthly transactions and volume. This data showed that M-PESA, despite its popularity and vast number of transactions per day, was actually moving a small amount of value, half of what moved through ATMs every day, and a pittance compared to the overall gross bank settlements. Again, this evidence showed that M-PESA was, in fact, still operating on the margins. This may have been because the Central Bank had limited the maximum transfer at roughly $625 – and the size of the average transfer was in the $25 range.

The Central Bank reaffirmed that its initial audit had been thorough, nothing had emerged to change its mind, and M-PESA could operate legally in Kenya. At the same time, the Central Bank declared its intention to fast track a bill being considered by Parliament, to allow banks to create an agent network. In a speech at MIT in 2010, the Governor of the Central Bank referred back to the audit. "I was told in 2008 that M-PESA was dangerous," Governor Njuguna Ndung'u said. "I asked why. My regulators convinced me it was safe."

THE NEW MOBILE MONEY PLAYING FIELD

Less than a month after the initial request for an audit, the then Permanent Secretary in the Ministry of Finance, Joseph Kinyua, announced that the audit by the Central Bank of M-PESA found the service safe and reliable. "I therefore reiterate that the Treasury and the Central Bank of Kenya are committed to promoting safe and efficient innovations that enhance access to financial services, thereby addressing the challenge of financial exclusion due to infrastructural constraints."

Mr. Kinyua authoritatively stated that, according to the audit report, there was no evidence to support the claims that the service was competing with commercial banks. "In any case, there is nothing wrong with competition as long as it is underpinned by a level playing field," he said. "CBK has placed the maximum limit of KShs 50,000 per M-PESA account per day and a transaction limit of KShs 35,000 per day in order to mitigate against settlement risk."

This affirmation was part of a coordinated effort with the Central Bank to give a clear signal to the market that M-PESA had been given a green light. Both the Ministry of Finance and the Central Bank took out a full page advertisement in *The Daily Nation*. Tellingly, one of the Bank's key public comments noted the 2006 FinAccess report on financial exclusion, pointing out that while few had access to banks, most had access to phones. The Central Bank's statement began with an endorsement of mobile telephony: "At the onset, the Bank welcomes innovation that has been introduced in Kenya's financial sector through the use of mobile telephony."

In addition, the Bank had gone beyond its initial audit to run an aging analysis of M-PESA accounts to see if people really were using them as de facto savings accounts. It found that the amount of money sitting in idle accounts was typically less than $2, nothing a bank would care about. Finally, to assuage Zain's concerns, the CBK noted that Zain was partnering with a commercial bank, and thus subject to a different review process. Shortly thereafter, Zain launched Zap!, and the banks began a rush to engage with M-PESA. The one month brouhaha over regulation had produced a clear playing field for business actors. As M-PESA was adding 12,000 customers a day, it paid to ride its coattails.

Two financial institutions had already jumped on the M-PESA bandwagon. Family Bank, a large and fast growing people's bank, introduced *Chapaa chap chap* ["money real quick"] in late 2007. Family Bank ATM cardholders could send money to their M-PESA accounts. The service eliminated a two step process of withdrawing money from an ATM then looking for an agent to deposit the money into M-PESA. The service charge was slightly higher than for regular ATM services, but clearly a convenience for those with accounts. From M-PESA's perspective, it added 650 ATMs to its growing network.

A few months before the audit, M-PESA had also signed an agreement with PesaPoint Ltd to allow M-PESA subscribers to withdraw money from their ATMs. PesaPoint is not a bank, but a system of ATMs that any bank holder can use to withdraw funds. As PesaPoint only had 110 ATMs, the impact was marginal, but a harbinger of what was coming. And, between Family Bank and PesaPoint, M-PESA had added 760 "automated agents" to its expanding network, at no cost to Safaricom.

A few months after the audit, Kenya Commercial Bank (KCB) connected to M-PESA. The largest bank in terms of assets, KCB has a presence in Kenya, Uganda, Tanzania, Rwanda and South Sudan, a network that could eventually enable M-PESA agents to access cash across a large swath of East Africa.

As part of the partnership, KCB became the second super agent, designed to ease M-PESA agent access to e-float. Authorized agents could instantly access e-float once they made cash deposits at any KCB branch. Prior to this agreement, agents had to deposit cash into the M-PESA Holding Company bank account at Commercial Bank of Africa. To convert e-money to cash (withdrawal), agents had to initiate a request on the M-PESA system, which then would go through an internal process before the money was transferred to the agent's bank account (likely at another commercial bank) through an Electronic Funds Transfer (EFT). That could easily take two days.

Safaricom and KCB had tested the service with 20 agencies and 16 KCB branches in different parts of the country. Following the successful pilot, 143 KCB branches across the nation were trained how to interact with M-PESA agents eager to "rebalance."

Barclays Bank soon followed, signing on as a super agent, and then Eco Bank, with a presence in 30 African countries (although only 19 branches in Kenya). Eco also introduced M-PESA bulk payment services to enable corporate and institutional clients to pay their employees via M-PESA. With the big hitters coming on board, a new financial ecosystem was taking shape. Banks that had months earlier tried to shut down M-PESA and painted them as a competitor with unfair advantages, were taking advantage of M-PESA's huge customer base and monetary flows to increase their own business and transaction fees. Super agents were sitting on piles of cash, mirroring e-float in the system. At the same time, they were helping agents rebalance more quickly and provide cash and e-float on demand – for a transaction fee.

But those deals were just setting the table for Equity Bank. Before M-PESA came along, Equity Bank was the meteoric banking performer in Kenya. A "building society" that helped finance houses, Equity had roughly 100,000 customers in 2001. Equity became a bank in 2004 and had attracted 5 million account holders by 2010. Equity held more than half (56%) of all bank accounts in Kenya; the other 42 banks had 44%! While most banks fought over high-end customers, Equity had developed products for the "common man," promoting financial inclusion by attracting low- and mid-income account holders, and even deploying a 4WD Land Rover as a rural bank that roamed from village to village. [DFID, the British development agency that seeded M-PESA and FSD, also funded Equity's rural outreach.] Needless to say, Equity saw M-PESA as encroaching on its hard won turf.

Equity's CEO, James Mwangi, like Safaricom's former CEO Joseph, is a charismatic CEO with a great track record. Joseph had 17,500 agents to Mwangi's 165 branches and 550 ATMs. But the two fast growing institutions are symbiotic, for most Equity account holders use M-PESA, and a third of M-PESA subscribers have accounts at Equity. It was only natural that they connect, although complex because they were in many ways fighting over "ownership" of the same customers.

In 2010, Equity Bank partnered with Safaricom, allowing M-PESA customers to access their money from Equity's 550 ATMs. Unlike the Family Bank arrangement, an M-PESA subscriber didn't need an Equity account to withdraw money. On the M-PESA menu, a user selects Withdraw Funds, puts in agent code 286286 (treating the ATM like a regular agent), then a Safaricom phone number, and receives a code. Input the code into an Equity ATM and out tumbles the cash. This really was the first step in putting hitherto unbanked Kenyans in direct contact with a bank. Meanwhile, M-PESA put another 550 ATM notches on its belt (it now had 1,310, the vast majority of ATMs in Kenya), as well as turning its already extended hours into a 24 hour service.

"Nine million people are now using M-PESA and they can go into Equity ATMs and draw money. It will be very convenient for the subscribers as they will not have to hear the 'we have no float' excuse," Joseph said, suggesting that customer complaints on liquidity had become an issue for Safaricom. A year after the contentious audit, the biggest bank in Kenya had created a win-win arrangement with M-PESA.

To reassure M-PESA agents, many of whom now depended on the M-PESA agency business for their daily livelihood, Joseph laid out the facts: "We have about 550 Equity ATMs in the country and more than 15,000 M-PESA agents across the country. Therefore, these (Equity ATMs) are a very small proportion and the agents will definitely continue serving people and will continue making money." Equity's Mwangi added that the bank would also be a cashing point for the agents, acting as a super agent that would distribute e-float. Rebalancing was a pain point for agents, and Equity was part of the solution. Of course, like other bank super agents, Equity was signing up for a fairly brisk business with potentially huge sums of cash in every transaction, on which it was earning transaction fees.

M-KESHO: A BANKING PRODUCT FOR THE UNBANKED

What Joseph didn't tell his agents was that Equity would soon be building its own agent network to compete with M-PESA agents, thanks to new banking regulations that had passed parliament as part of the Finance Act of 2009. But that would come only after another more ambitious joint project between Safaricom and Equity – M-KESHO (*kesho* is a Swahili word for tomorrow, in this case referring to building a better future).

M-KESHO was hashed out through a series of one on one meetings between Joseph and Mwangi. You can imagine these two Goliaths of Kenyan business circling each other with caution. The design process was slow but steady; the commercial negotiations somewhat more contentious. Equity felt all transaction fees should accrue to the bank; Safaricom felt its distribution channel would bring customers to the bank. Eventually, after a series of breakfast meetings between the CEOs, they worked out a deal. Unfortunately for the customer, both Safaricom and Equity are getting transaction fees.

"There was a lot of suspicion between the two companies," says Safaricom's Joseph. "The revenue we made on M-KESHO had to be 50-50. If they made more than we made, we had to get another costing pricing formula. James ([Mwangi, CEO of Equity] and I said, 'We are going to do this,' and the teams said, 'It's not possible and it cannot be done,' and we said, 'Well, we're just going to do it.'" And they did.

If M-PESA is a money-transfer solution, M-KESHO is a true mobile-banking solution. In one sense,

M-KESHO goes a step or two beyond the other ATM arrangements M-PESA had spawned; Equity account holders cannot only withdraw money from an ATM, but send money directly from their accounts to M-PESA – and vice versa. Now, you don't have to visit an agent – or an ATM – to do business with the bank.

That was a marginal improvement, but M-KESHO was revolutionary in this sense: non-account holders could open an Equity savings account and deposit as little as KShs 100 ($1.25), on which they would earn 1% interest. Not much, but this was truly an opportunity for the unbanked to join the banked, to move from the informal and quasi-formal financial sector to the formal sector.

CEOs Joseph and Mwangi, in their joint introduction, did their best to outdo each other. Joseph crowed that M-KESHO had the "potential to introduce a savings culture to Kenya." Mwangi crowed that if all 11 million M-PESA subscribers were to save KShs 10,000 ($125), it would be a "colossal" mobilization equal to KShs 120 billion. That was a businessman's fantasy: in 2010, all Equity deposits equalled KShs 104 billion! But Mwangi saw a bright *Kesho*.

Savings was just one aspect of M-KESHO, although the easiest to explain and execute. [The 2009 FinAccess survey found that 90% of Kenyans understood the term "savings," while only 50% understood the term "credit," and even fewer "equity."] M-KESHO also included a microcredit component, which would allow a non-Equity Bank customer to take out a small loan (up to KShs 5000) based on a review of six months of M-PESA and M-KESHO transactions. In other words, M-PESA could be used to establish a credit history. Equity Bank, true to its name, was giving those without collateral a way to build credit. M-KESHO also offered micro insurance against accidents.

In the first four months, 650,000 customers opened M-KESHO accounts. The uptake was faster than that of M-PESA, but nearly 90% of M-KESHO customers were already Equity Bank customers just looking for an easier way to move money between the bank and M-PESA. And the transaction volume was low. The appeal of M-KESHO was not readily apparent to M-PESA subscribers, many of whom eyed banks warily, and for whom a marginal interest on savings was less important than safe storage and quick transfers, which M-PESA already allowed. Double transaction fees didn't help. The long term success of M-KESHO is far from assured; it may in retrospect be viewed as a first and somewhat clumsy effort to mix and match two very different products and two very different customer bases.

But, for Equity Bank, M-KESHO represents a learning experience. Since the Finance Act of 2009, which for the first time ever gave banks the green light to operate through agents outside of their bank branches, banks are beginning to build their own networks. "The expansion we see in Kenya is more to use delivery channels offered by telecoms and agencies," CEO Mwangi told reporters after announcing record profits in 2010. "Instead of branches, we open an agent in every village."

However, it will be more difficult for banks to build a network than it was for Safaricom. First, they have to offer better deals than Safaricom. Second, they cannot "share" M-PESA agents, because M-PESA agencies have signed exclusivity contracts with Safaricom. Third, banks cannot create their own exclusive agents, according to the law, so any network one bank builds could potentially be used by another. Was the Central Bank creating another double standard?

The Central Bank, which approves bank agents on a case by case basis, requires that an agent must be a commercial entity and have been in business for 18 months. (See Chapter 7, "Change Is Not Easy.") Thus, the Central Bank sees the Post Office, shops, supermarkets and pharmacies as potential agent locations. Both Postbank and the Postal Corporation of Kenya (PCK) are rolling out point of sale terminals in post offices, to allow for easy money transfer; every Postbank customer will be converted to a card-based system. In 2011, when the Central Bank released the agent banking guidelines, more than 10,000 bank agents were approved, roughly 5,000 for Equity Bank, who were non-exclusive to any one bank.

Taken together with agents for new mobile money services YuCash, Orange Money and Bharti Airtel, this meant that there were more than 40,000 agents in Kenya, when five years earlier there had been barely 1,000 ATMs.

A NEW FINANCIAL SECTOR EMERGES

The disruption of the banks has been good for the financial sector in Kenya. "The Kenyan financial sector has been rapidly transformed in the last five years, as witnessed by the emergence of new financial products facilitated by advancement of information technology," says Governor Ndung'u. "Such products have increased financial services to the majority of Kenyans who were previously unbanked and who belong to the bottom billion of the world."

The number of branches increased from 534 in 2005 to 1030 in 2010, widely distributed across the country. In fact, growth in the branch network favoured rural areas, with 140% growth versus 68% in urban areas, according to Central Bank data. At the same time, the share of the three largest banks declined, implying enhanced competition in the sector.

Bank deposits also increased markedly, from 2.55 million in 2005 to nearly 12 million in 2010. The bulk of the increase occurred amongst micro accounts. Total assets in the banking sector increased at roughly the same rate.

Two metrics show just how positive the development of M-PESA has been for banks. Since 2007, when M-PESA was introduced, the amount of currency outside banks has been declining steadily, as a percentage of overall money supply and reserve currency. Central Bank Governor Ndung'u cites this as a signal of increased financial intermediation, implying that many who had previously been excluded from banking services were now using more appropriate financial instruments.

As Ndemo, the Permanent Secretary of Kenya's ICT Ministry notes: "Mobile money has brought money that used to be under the pillows into circulation. And I would attribute the increased liquidity in the banks to greater circulation of that resource. When there is liquidity in the banks, it impacts the interest rate, because banks want to lend that money." Indeed, the expansion of Kenya's money supply based on lending has been on an upward trajectory since 2007, indicating that banks are lending their excess liquidity.

Aside from the business battle between banks and MNOs, how amazing that they were fighting over a customer that had been essentially invisible to both banks and telecoms a decade earlier. One winner is clear: the Kenyan people, especially those poor and unbanked at the "base of the pyramid."

****

Kiogothe has been a makanga – public service vehicle co-driver – since he was 18 years old. He's up by 4 a.m. and not in bed until late, sometimes past midnight. Makangas are known to be very rowdy and ruthless, a fact that Kiogothe confirms. After collecting money from passengers, he would instill fear in them with rough talk and physical gestures, so that no one would rob him. Behaving tough, he says, was a requirement for the job.

When he closed out around midnight, he would pay his driver a salary for the day and carry the rest of his money home. The next day he would deposit the money in his employer's account at midday, when there is not much matatu (small bus) business. He'd stand in line for at least 30 minutes because the banks were busy at midday.

Kiogothe often lost his whole day's earnings to robbers. His next day salary would be used to pay off his employer, who grew tired of his antics and tales. Kiogothe had to quit the job and started selling second-hand shoes in a market. But he couldn't make ends meet and went back to the makanga business. This time, he was much more aggressive defending himself against robbers, but was jailed several times for hurting people and paid large fines.

That was before M-PESA. Now, Kiogothe performs his duties with respect for his customers. By 8 in the morning, several M-PESA shops have opened. He deposits all earnings up to that hour. As the day progresses, he deposits money along the way. As passengers board his matatu, he goes to one of the M-PESA shops and deposits the money. During midday, when there is no business, Kiogothe now relaxes instead of visiting the bank, waiting for the evening when business is booming.

Around 8pm, when the last M-PESA shop closes, he makes his last deposit. He keeps any other money that he may earn from there on and deposits it the next morning. Once home, using his mobile phone, he transfers money from his M-PESA account to his employer's M-PESA account. With M-PESA, he keeps his accounts straight and his earnings safe. And he stays out of jail.

Chapter 4

IMPACT AT THE BASE OF THE PYRAMID

Mathandu is a shoemaker in the Mukuru Kwa Njenga slum. He earns KSh 200 ($2) per day. He has three wives and nine children, between 1 and 15 years of age, who live on a rural farm 250 miles away. He sends money home frequently to support his huge family. In Mukuru Kwa Njenga, Mathundu lives in a tin-walled structure, which he shares with a friend who is a shoe cleaner.

In his village, his wives farm small plots of land divided amongst them. These plots produce food for subsistence, but not enough to sell. Mathundu provides money for clothes and other basic needs. His first two children are in a local missionary primary school and need school materials.

Before M-PESA, Mathundu sent money home with his friends. Some weren't honest, and either didn't deliver the money, or pocketed some of it. Mathudu then resorted to postal services, but this proved to be very expensive as he was sending small amounts every week.

At times, when he didn't make enough money to send using PostaPay, one of his wives would travel to the slum to get money. This forced Mathundu to travel home at the end of every week. The transport costs were as bad as those of PostaPay, but at least he visited with his family.

When he adopted M-PESA, he was able to send money with a few clicks on his mobile phone – and *incur few transaction costs. Kagure, the youngest of his three wives, reports receiving KShs 500 ($5) per month since she subscribed to M-PESA, a big increase and a vital one, as such remittances constitute a substantial part of her household income.*

****

Send money home. From the beginning, M-PESA was fuelled by a relentless wave of remittances from the city to rural areas. Men – mostly young, banked and successful, but also hard-working, $2 a day *jua kali* (day labourers) and other urban migrants – were sending money home to women in villages – wives, mothers, grandmothers, and aunts. The women, many of whom hadn't used phones before, eagerly adopted them and subscribed to M-PESA. You didn't need to be a subscriber to receive money, but if you were not the sender you paid a surcharge. As long as there were agents in the right place at the right time – and Safaricom spent hours poring over transaction data to determine the right place and right time – the M-PESA system was a well-oiled electronic payment machine. It was revolutionary. Suddenly, the flows reversed.

During the post-election violence in 2008, when 1,500 were killed, banks were closed, roads were blocked by rioting youth, and sections of the railway were dismantled. Urban migrants, who had come to the city to work and send money home, were desperate for cash and even airtime, both aids to escaping the horrific ethnic violence. Forget speed, convenience, safety – they just needed cash any way they could get it. M-PESA payments started coming from the village to the city, particularly the large urban slum settlement of Kibera, a city within the city of Nairobi. Agents found that urban customers were making withdrawals instead of deposits. Once desperate for e-float, agents now scrambled to find cash with the banks closed.

Olga Morawczynski, an anthropologist who studied money flows between Kibera and the farming village of Bukura in Western Kenya, observed this dramatic shift. The shift was temporary, but significant – money was flowing at the so-called base of the pyramid, from the poor to the poor. Allowing money to flow electronically, rather than physically, eradicated the space and time barriers to money transfer. And people who had been recipients, merely withdrawing cash, were now depositing and sending it. M-PESA had been a one-way transaction rail; it was now two-way.

Every year, more and more of the very poor are using M-PESA. The Kenya Economic Update, published by the World Bank in December, 2010, notes that 40% of the poorest quintile of Kenyans used mobile money, far below the 90% level in the top two quintiles, but a huge increase amongst the poor, particularly women. And, while M-PESA usage is still highest amongst urban dwellers, 60% of adults in rural regions had adopted M-PESA. The increasing uptake at the base of the pyramid has multiple positive spinoff effects, as people invent new ways to utilize M-PESA, and new products are designed to leverage the growing network of poor people.

CASH IS THE ENEMY

In a cash economy, cash is king, but cash is also the enemy. This is a signature concept of Ignacio Mas, formerly a senior advisor in the Financial Services for the Poor group at the Bill & Melinda Gates Foundation, now an independent consultant. Cash is the enemy of governments, which must replace ripped notes by printing and distributing new currency; it is the enemy of bill payers, who must waste half days queuing to pay water and electric bills, or getting bank cheques to pay school tuition; it is the enemy of businesses, which have no easy and verifiable way to offer credit to customers or pay suppliers in advance, or to pay their workers in cash, which restricts them to doing business in small geographic circles.

But cash is the most formidable enemy of the poor. Cash is difficult to store and certainly to save; and the transaction costs are prohibitive. That's why, in many parts of the developing world, the idea of interest on savings is irrelevant; people often pay as much as 30% to get others to safely store money for them. That is a lower transaction cost than the alternative, which might mean seeing the money disappear altogether.

The poor depend on cash but it is the enemy; the poor have little money but lead complex financial lives; the poor have low cash balances but move large amounts of cash every day, week and month. The many conundrums of the poor and cash have been increasingly well documented in recent years through in-depth financial diaries, notably in the book, *Portfolios of the Poor*. Many of the ideas in the book were first introduced by Stuart Rutherford (one of *Portfolios'* authors) in his foundational 1999 essay, "The Poor and Their Money", based on his then 20 years of research with the poor in many parts of the world:

"If you live in an urban slum or in a straw hut in a village, finding a safe place to store savings is not easy. Bank notes tucked into rafters, buried in the earth, rolled inside hollowed-out bamboo, or thrust into clay piggy banks, can be lost or stolen or blown away or may just rot. Certainly their value will decline, because of inflation. But the physical risks are the least of the problem. Much tougher is keeping the cash safe from the many claims on it – claims by relatives who have fallen on hard times, by importunate neighbours, by hungry or sick children or alcoholic husbands and by landlords, creditors and beggars. Finally, even when you do have a little cash left over at the day's end, if you don't have somewhere safe to put it you'll most probably spend it in some trivial way or other. I have lost count of the number of women who have told me how hard it is to save at home, and how much they would value a safe, simple way to save. Unable to save at home, and unable to go to remote unfriendly banks, they trust their savings to unlicensed, informal, peripatetic collectors. When they find one that they can trust, time and time again, they are willing to pay a high price (as much as 30% a year) to have that collector take away their savings and store them safely until needed."

SAVING IN THE SLUMS

Kibera is one of the largest slums in Africa, an informal settlement on government-owned land – which is not well serviced by the government with streets, electricity, water or sewers. In Kibera, as in other poor areas, M-PESA helps people to store and save money. While there is some debate about the extent to which mobile phones are used for any savings, let alone long term savings, there is little debate that they are used for short term storage, which is often transferred into larger group pools to amass lump sums.

For low income Kenyans, concludes a report by Financial Sector Deepening, M-PESA seems to "hit that sweet spot for saving that keeps funds close enough to use in an emergency, but also imposes a cost on withdrawals that serves as an effective commitment feature preventing haphazard withdrawal for consumption spending – something that makes mobile money a hit for the poor."

Kibera is at once one of the world's most depressing and most uplifting spots. Depressing because it is hard to imagine life in an "informal settlement" of over 250,000 people (the actual number is probably much, much higher, but there are no records), living without running water or toilets or sewage, packed together in tin and mud shacks with dirt floors and little air, stuck inside a maze of twisty passages with no escape from your neighbours or thugs or the smell of human and animal waste or the heavy air, smoky from cooking fires. The Mombasa-Kisumu train en route to Uganda roars through every day scattering children playing on the tracks. Aside from a few battery-operated lights and illegally spliced electric lines, Kibera is dark at night.

But Kibera is also uplifting for the civilisation it has built. Its electronics shops and beauty shops and clothing shops and furniture stalls and brilliant graffiti art on the roofs, so those above know they exist, for its joyous human spirit, what novelist William Faulkner referred to in his Nobel acceptance speech as the "indomitable spirit of man," for the determination of its people to gather themselves and somehow move forward in life.

We tend to think of the poor as a block of people who go through life poor, living in a separate universe where suffering knows no boundaries. But for many people, poverty is a temporary condition. People move in and out of poverty, or out altogether, depending on health and circumstances and luck and how hard they work. And one way to do that is by mobilizing money.

Lukas Alube grew up in Kibera, got an education (library science) and got out – but is now working there under the auspices of the Anglican Church to help residents mobilize money. He formed a savings group called Jipange Sasa (Plan Now), noteworthy for its reliance on M-PESA as a transactional tool. M-PESA speeds up collections and bookkeeping, increases the amount saved in group funds, and has even been used to invest in the stock market. "This is not a place you work to improve," says Alube. "People here must get out and for that they must fight."

Alube has started at least 15 savings groups, and many in turn have spread the gospel and knowledge to others. Charles Oronje, for example, a skilled furniture maker who lives in Kibera, started the Gatwikera Railway Savings Club in 2004; three years later, the group counted 54 members, many of whom disappeared during the post-election violence. "In my own groups, I have to start very simply," Lukas told Kim Wilson, a microfinance specialist at The Fletcher School, who visited Kibera. "With 'dear ones' [the poorest of the poor] I must begin at the beginning. These members are often new to Kibera, are out of money, frightened, and a little desperate."

The basic group is a merry-go-round, a savings mechanism used by the poor around the world, even in developed countries. Each member puts in a fixed amount every week, and every week one member gets the whole pot. Around it goes, until everyone gets a turn. It requires discipline – the same amount deposited every week – but the payoff is fairly immediate and can be large, depending on the size of the group. If you were to be first or second to take the pot, the sum would really be a loan that you would then repay every week until the group disbanded or started over again. It's an easy way of mobilizing what Rutherford calls a "lump sum," and a clear example of why saving and borrowing are simply flip sides of the same coin.

The problem is that many people in savings groups can't regularly attend meetings due to work – many work night shifts in Nairobi, for example. So Jipange Sasa lets people contribute through M-PESA. A deposit collector responsible for a segment of the group receives the money, and forwards it to a group account managed by the treasurer. If the collector receives cash, he deposits it with an M-PESA agent and forwards it to the treasurer. The transfer fee can amount to 15% or more of the bulk cash – but that "negative interest rate" is cheaper than the higher transaction cost of attending a weekly meeting. And it is more reliable than trying to hold onto money for two weeks before contributing. Each week, a member of the management committee visits an M-PESA agent and withdraws the money for that week's "beneficiary."

Once the merry-go-round concept is fully functional, Alube introduces more sophisticated vehicles for savings, such as the idea of investing the savings. That includes buying unit trusts (much like a mutual fund) through a trust manager such as Zimele Asset Management, which trades securities on the Nairobi Stock Exchange. With M-PESA, groups can send as little as $3 per month to top up their Zimele accounts. People in Kibera, often living on pennies a day, are investing in the stock market as a route out of Kibera. This would not be possible without M-PESA, without people's trust in the system, without the innovation that it inspires.

Just as M-PESA encourages urban migrants to send money home more often, Alube says people save more often. M-PESA enforces discipline because the saver has no excuse for the collector, whose phone is always on, ready to receive a payment. Cash dissipates much more easily, spent on alcohol or other impulse purchases. Receiving payments in advance means group meetings are not spent discussing payments and bookkeeping, but can address larger, long-term issues such as burial savings, school fees and neighbourhood safety.

JUA KALI

Most people in Kibera work in the "informal sector." The term "informal sector" was popularized by a 1972 study of Kenya, but Kenyans have another term for the sector: *jua kali*, which literally means "under the hot sun." *Jua kali* describes casual labourers and small enterprising businesspeople that operate in small shops, creating products and fixing others: metallic artefacts, wooden furniture, clay products, and animal-skin decors. Originally the term was restricted to artisans, but now it includes many other day labourers, including market vendors, auto mechanics and small-scale farmers. Many have graduated from high school or even from technical colleges but cannot find work in the formal sector. *Jua kali*, of course, are not restricted to Kibera in Nairobi, nor are they necessarily urban – many live in rural areas.

An estimated 8 million Kenyans (nearly half of Kenya's 18 million workforce) are jua kali, the vast majority of whom lack access to formal financial services. M-PESA has filled that void, and helped jua kali to streamline transactions with their suppliers and customers (as well as save). Jua kali no longer need to close their shops and travel to pay a distant supplier and arrange delivery; they simply M-PESA the money to the supplier who then sends the goods. For rural jua kali in particular, who are more distant from suppliers, M-PESA is a huge time saver.

ex helps small businesses supply chain

Money also flows to the jua kali from distributors, or middlemen. The half-acre coffee farmer, the two-cow milk producer and the two-acre tea grower – all bring their produce to a collection point before it's taken for processing and distribution. Jua kali are typically paid in cash monthly or weekly, which presents a logistical problem for distributors. "Moving cash down the value chain to thousands of small producers is very difficult," says Nick Hughes, who initiated M-PESA in 2003 when he was at Vodafone. "Now, a group of women has started running a payments system through M-PESA that much more efficiently moves money up and down the chain." Distributors lower their costs; producers receive money more quickly. And it is safely stored on a phone in their village, rather than picked up in a market town and quickly spent.

M-PESA's bulk payment feature allows employers to sign up with a bank and deposit a lump sum, which is then automatically sent to employees' M-PESA accounts. For the bank, the process is similar to sending e-float to agents in exchange for cash. Safaricom provides a simple application that connects to the core banking system. The employer absorbs the transaction fee, split between Safaricom and the bank. The employee gets his or her money in electronic form, without having to travel to a central station and wait in line.

The Mumias Sugar Company, for example, has started paying its 13,000 cane cutters by M-PESA or Airtel Money (offered through Bharti Airtel). In the past, cane cutters had to abandon work for a day or two and line up at pay points, which cut into their work hours and resulted in lower cane supplies at the factory. Cutters who don't own phones can take out "soft loans" of KShs 2000 from the company to buy phones and establish mobile money accounts. "It is a nice one I can say, it doesn't need you to walk for long to go receive your salary," said Wekesa, a cane cutter with the company. "It happens everywhere at any time, and it has also minimized some of the burdens when you want to send some money home."

"Cane cutters are our key partners and as a company we continuously look for ways through which they can efficiently manage their incomes just like other people in gainful employment," said the then Mumias Sugar Managing Director Evans Kidero. "By introducing such a service the cutters will develop a savings culture without having to trek long distances."

The ease of making payments via M-PESA has also led to the creation of the Mbao Pension Scheme for jua kali, established in 2010 by Kenya National Jua kali Co-operative Society. Subscribers send at least KShs 20 a day via M-PESA to earn a pension after their retirement. Edward Odundo, Managing Director of the Retirement Benefits Authority, expects 1.5 million artisans to contribute by 2013, which would make the plan the largest in the country, with the possibility of expanding to other countries in the region. As of 2010, seven out of 10 in the informal sector had no retirement or pension plans, making the Mbao scheme an extremely positive development.

CASH CIRCULATES IN REMOTE VILLAGES

Once normal urban-rural, Kibera-Bukura remittance patterns took hold again after the post-election violence subsided, one of anthropologist Morawczynski's more stunning findings was the impact on household income in the Bukura village. Three-quarters noted an increase in income, and the increase ranged from 5% to 30%. Many other researchers have since confirmed similar findings in many other areas. The increase was a result of money being sent more frequently, in smaller amounts. By sending smaller amounts more frequently, urban migrants were sending more money home. And rural recipients were saving the cash. They no longer needed to pay for transport costs to urban centres, where most of the money transfer services were located. Instead, recipients made the withdrawal directly from agents in Bukura. In the past, even requesting money required a long trip to the local market town to send a letter by post. And the stamp to send the letter wasn't free! The combination of increased transfers and lower transactions costs, along with instantaneous communications, translated into more money in the village, which of course has sparked local economies.

As M-PESA remittances redistribute money from urban to rural areas, savings are more productively allocated across households, families and businesses. Instead of shopping in the market town where they once got cash, women now withdraw cash from agents in their villages and spend it there. Increased cash from remittances allows farmers to hire more casual labour, which in turn keeps more money circulating in the village in a virtuous circle: more money in circulation with lower transaction costs means more transactions and less seepage of money outside the community.

In the past, money in a village was basically tucked in a mattress, or some equivalent. It did not flow; it was invisible. Now, e-money is stored in a phone, and that increases its velocity; it circulates to businesses, farmers, and schools and finds its way into the bank. When you can control cash and convert it to e-money and back at will, cash is more ally than enemy.

A study of community level effects of M-PESA by the Iris Center at the University of Maryland found it was possible to see gains even for non-users. In Murang'a, a district in the Central province, 75 kilometres from Nairobi, the Managing Director of an M-PESA outlet said he has seen an expansion of businesses due to M-PESA, namely fish buyers and a woman who buys cakes and sweets using M-PESA and sells them to area hotels. A tomato vendor from Katulani sees people go to the M-PESA vendor first and then come to buy food. He says business has doubled since an M-PESA shop moved into the shopping centre.

Outside Kitui town, shopkeepers are using M-PESA to order seeds delivered to their shops, which are close to farms. Farmers who receive remittances can buy seeds and other inputs in a timely fashion, which increases agricultural productivity and results in more food moving through the markets. A Murang'a agent says that many of her customers receive money quickly and plant early and fully, whereas in the past they might not have the seeds on time. With more money circulating, many vendors order more food in advance and pay for it on time.

This virtuous circle frees money for other agricultural inputs, and even labour. A study on the impact of M-PESA concludes that M-PESA is associated with increases in employment, but that these are almost exclusively changes in farm employment. "One possible explanation," write authors Isaac Mbiti and David Weil, "is that the increased resource flows are channelled towards farming, thus boosting the demand for labour and increasing employment."

One of the biggest benefits of M-PESA is the speed with which people can request and receive remittances in a "rescue" situation. For many Kenyans, especially those who produce much of their own food, life on $2 a day is often quite manageable, given the various hedging, saving and borrowing the poor employ to navigate through life. But it is the unexpected shocks, such as crop loss due to drought or flooding, health issues, and job loss, which are difficult to overcome without a regular flow of income or ample savings. Receiving a remittance early on can prevent further follow-on shocks, such as childhood sickness and missed school, inability to repay debts, or failure to replant a second crop.

For many Kenyans, food security is the biggest day-to-day concern. An estimated 3.8 million Kenyans are highly or extremely food insecure (USAID, 2009); according to the latest Global Hunger Index, more Kenyans are in need of emergency food aid today than 20 years ago. Food consumption, in particular, fluctuates with income – but M-PESA users are better able to put food on the table in a given week. This is particularly true for households that live close to agents. A three year study of 3,000 M-PESA and non-M-PESA users, by Tavneet Suri (MIT) and William Jack (Georgetown), concludes that M-PESA users suffer almost no negative effects from shocks, while non-users as a group reduce overall consumption of goods by 7% (and most of the decline is food).

Increased food security has a positive impact on human capital, as people eat better and attend school more often. You can't measure this the way you measure a retailer's balance sheet, but development economists know that over time an improvement in human capital means an improvement in the quality of life and better access to life's opportunities.

THE LAST MILE/FIRST MILE CONUNDRUM

If most of the world's poor are rural, the poorest of the poor are often those living in the most remote areas, often reachable only by footpaths, which put them beyond the reach of most products and services from government, development agencies or private vendors, whether it's malaria nets or bars of soap. No electricity, banks, phones, roads, hospitals. It costs too much to reach too few people to build a reliable infrastructure. Even inner city or peri-urban slums, such as Kibera, where providers could theoretically reach a million people, qualify as "remote," in that they are walled off from the grid that the developed world connects to and takes for granted.

These difficult to reach areas are considered part of the "last mile" – originally a telecom term that described the difficulty of making the final connection from transformers to individual households. From the vantage point of the individual, the last mile is really the first mile. And it's only fitting that telecom operators have begun to solve the problem that has long befuddled the industry.

Mobile operators were the first service providers to extend networks into remote areas, sometimes using diesel-powered cell stations, but increasingly wind and solar-powered stations that are more efficient to operate. Access to communications networks connected people to each other, to nearby villages and market towns, and to far-flung relatives. Those mobile networks, of course, have now morphed into conduits for mobile money services.

M-PESA was initially conceived as a way to provide financial access for the poor, but most of its initial success was driven by middle and upper income urban dwellers. They are the people putting money into the M-PESA system. But M-PESA's biggest impact has been on the poor, who are more disconnected from the world's grids than any other segment, for whom cash is the enemy – and for whom e-money is an ally.

"What's interesting to see is that M-PESA was not a tool for the base of the pyramid, it was meant for the middle of the pyramid, but what's so special is that it trickled down so quickly," says Wolfgang Fengler, lead economist for the World Bank in Nairobi. "It's good if it starts from the top as long as it trickles down very quickly."

****

Atieno is a middle-aged woman in the rural, Western town of Kogero. She is chairperson of a women's self help group, which is actively engaged in fish mongering from the local lake. Sometimes, the women were sending their excess processed fish to relatives in Nairobi, where they got better prices. Atieno coordinated all the business with her mobile phone.

Customers in Nairobi advised the women to open a bank account so they could pay directly, rather than sending money by cargo trucks. Atieno went to the nearest bank branch, which is 35 kilometres away. But their application was rejected because the group had no valid registration certificate and utility bill, standard documentation for bank KYC regulations.

Not long after this rejection, the group adopted M-PESA. Atieno informs customers that the fish is on the way, a 10 hour trip. When the fish reach Nairobi, the recipient weighs them, informs Atieno of the receipt – and then sends payment via M-PESA. Atieno disburses the money to group members, after deducting overhead costs.

The Kogero women now have a fulltime fish business that they rely on for their livelihoods. And, they are planning on starting a more formal firm dedicated to national fish distribution.

Chapter 5
INCHING TOWARDS "FINANCIAL INCLUSION"

Christabel Nyamweya, known as Chris, is a young businesswoman in Syokimau, a residential suburb on the outskirts of Nairobi, in Machakos district. She is married with a baby daughter. Many people have bought property in Syokimau and are building beautiful family houses. Most of the landowners don't have time to supervise their projects during the week, let alone facilitate the supply of material and equipment needed by workers on site.

This is the market gap that Chris is now filling. She was employed, like many of the homeowners, but quit her job in 2008 to start Benwood Enterprises, a family business run with her husband. She specialises in providing construction consulting services, supply and renting of construction material and equipment.

In a typical month, Chris interacts with about 15 clients, delivering equipment, picking up material, providing advice, signing up contracts and gathering payments. Chris moves around a lot in a day on her motorbike, covering about 100 kilometres a day.

She began her business when M-PESA was just taking off. At first, neither she nor most of her customers were M-PESA users. To illustrate how cash is the enemy and how low money velocity affected her business, she would start off with KShs 240,000 on a Monday, buying equipment that she would rent to three clients. She expected to receive Kshs 40,000 per client for the service. The equipment would stay at clients' sites for the entire month. Since most of the owners worked out of town during the week, she had to wait for the weekend to collect cash payment of Kshs 120,000. Sometimes she had to wait even longer. She depended on these payments to serve other clients, pay her bills and run her household. "When payments were delayed, I felt like I was going to faint," says Chris. "My life and business depend on cash flow. I need the payment as soon as I have delivered the goods."

With M-PESA, she expects payments a day after delivery! And her clients know it. After all, they can access M-PESA agents near their offices. With the KShs 120,000, Chris buys equipment for another client (80,000), pays her bills (20,000), saves (5,000), services her loan (12,000) and makes a contribution to her siblings' school fees (tuition, books, uniforms, etc.).

Another huge transformation for her business was M-KESHO [the joint Safaricom-Equity Bank savings/ credit product]. Before, she had two accounts at Equity Bank, a savings and a checking account. The nearest branch is 5 KM from her house, a 45-minute round trip. She signed up for M-KESHO to facilitate faster banking. She presses a few buttons on her phone to move the money to M-KESHO – into her savings account and her loan account. "In less than two minutes, I have banked anytime, anywhere. Within two minutes I have serviced my loans, paid my supplier balance, deposited my savings, sent my sibling her school fees, paid my employees. That's amazing!"

Thanks to M-KESHO, Chris's credit rating improved and she qualified for a loan to buy a pickup truck, a first for her business. Her credit rating improved *because she banks more and does more transactions through the bank. Before, she postponed deposits until they had accumulated enough to justify the trip to the bank. In many cases, she opted to make cash payments to her suppliers and workers and only take her loan payments and savings to the bank. Many business transactions went unrecorded and her bank didn't rate her credit highly.*

"Were it not for M-PESA and M-KESHO, I would not have received a loan to buy a vehicle for the business. Never! My business would not have grown."

****

There was currency along the East African coast in the early 19th century (silver coins called Thalers), but it was used mostly by Greek, European and Indian traders, and never circulated among Africans in the interior. It wasn't until 1896, when Indian workers building the Kenya-Uganda railway were paid in Indian rupees, that money circulated around the interior of Kenya and Uganda, gaining credibility under the names *rupia* and *pesa*, the latter adopted from the Indian word for money, *paisa*.

In 1905, the Indian rupee was sanctioned as the official currency of the British East African Protectorate (BEAP) of Kenya and Uganda. In 1920, shortly after Kenya became a British "crown colony" and the BEAP was abolished, the shilling replaced the rupee as official currency, and remains so today. In 2007, mobile money took off successfully after a number of other unsuccessful initiatives, meaning that the shilling can be represented by an SMS message. Money need not be metal nor paper nor cowrie shell, but can be an electronic flash on a screen as long as there is trust that the bearer of the flash will be able to redeem it when needed or use it as a method of exchange.

The shift to mobile money, in theory, democratizes finance by increasing the density of access points (anyone who has a phone) and by reducing the cost of transacting (sending an SMS versus making a trip), both of which had restricted financial services to wealthier and more urban residents. Mobile money is helping to move people from informal to quasi-formal and formal financial services, some of which are quite new and innovative.

As we've seen, mobile money has greased remittances, sending money from point A to point B, from person to person, so that people without bank accounts or those who live at great distances from banks have ready access to cash – at lower cost and less time. Today, in fact, you can send money from any of more than 80,000 Western Union locations in 45 countries (or through its website) direct to a mobile phone in Kenya (and The Philippines, Malaysia and Canada). Thus, international remittances can be transferred at the speed of SMS and considerably lower transaction fees than a typical Western Union transfer. In 2010, Kenyans living outside their country sent home $642 million, a 5% increase over 2009.

But do these and other smoother transfers translate to financial inclusion? Beyond saving time and money in transfer costs and payment mechanisms, does mobile money help or allow the poor to better leverage money for productive purposes? Or is it just a convenience for those who are already banked, giving them just one more channel for their finances? The answer is probably yes on both counts, although the potential for inclusion is much greater than the reality. And it depends on whom you ask.

"M-PESA is not financial inclusion," says John Staley, Director of Mobile Banking and Payment Innovations at Equity Bank. "As long as you are paying a dollar for a transaction – that is not financial inclusion. What is Safaricom's biggest scratch card? One thousand shillings. But the biggest selling scratch card is 10 shillings. That tells me that most of their customers expend a lot of effort to get 10 shillings. What is the cost of an M-PESA transaction? Eighty shillings, combining transfer and withdrawal fees. The unbanked people who are using M-PESA are recipients.

"What M-PESA does is put money in one big trust account that the banks use to generate government and corporate bonds. So it is taking money away from the wananchi in small amounts and giving it to corporate entities."

Michael Klein, former chief economist for the IFC, who now lectures at several universities, has a different view: "Basic financial services seem to be of major benefit to poor people. The success of M-PESA in Kenya seems to indicate that basic payment services are perhaps the most important financial service for poor people."

Indeed, although most of the early adopters of M-PESA were previously banked and thus had some experience with financial services, as M-PESA matured it increasingly began to acquire customers who were completely unbanked. Research suggests that by early 2010, the percentage of unbanked adults who were using M-PESA increased from 25% to 50%. While they were more likely to be recipients of money transfers, they were connected to the e-money loop.

The truth is that branchless banking represents both less and more than financial inclusion. It is less because banks need to develop innovative financial products for low-income people if they want to become relevant to their customers. At the same time, branchless banking represents more than mere financial inclusion because the payment needs of all actors in the economy are much broader than their dealings with banks. Individuals, businesses and governments all benefit when money goes digital, and will do so even more when the payment channel becomes a utility that is universal and non-discriminatory. Financial inclusion is not just a function of access to a bank, but a function of new services for a new demographic.

THE POOR AND THEIR MONEY

One of the biggest hurdles to inclusion is providing people with the ability to mobilize money and save lump sums. Banks have not provided a solution, as the minimum balances required are too onerous to maintain for people who constantly shift money in and out of "pockets" (school, food, farm, emergencies, etc.). The poor and unbanked have instead created their own informal vehicles, such as merry-go-rounds, ASCAs (accumulated savings and credit associations) and ROSCAs (rotating savings and credit associations), aka susus and tontines, depending on the region of the world. These mechanisms are local, based on a high degree of trust, and flexible. They work best when people stick to a regular schedule for savings and withdrawals, but forgives slips in regularity without punishing the offenders.

At this point there is some evidence that M-PESA is being used for savings, usually as a short term storage mechanism rather than a long term, lump sum mechanism. An FSD study in late 2010, for example, found that the average balance held on M-PESA accounts had risen fivefold (to nearly $13) since a Central Bank audit the previous year. (The mean held in accounts is probably in the $3 range, according to most surveys.) Interest is not earned on deposits, and there is no capacity for borrowing, but M-PESA is clearly superior to many alternatives, such as the metaphorical "mattress." More importantly, since the Central Bank ruling in favour of M-PESA in January 2009, when banks decided to jump on the e-money bandwagon, banks have been building their own networks of agents to spread banking services far beyond branches. Branch density or lack thereof, was always a clear limitation to financial services for the poor.

These are all indicators that more people have access to more and better financial services. Money is moving faster and sticking in poorer and more remote regions longer, sparking local commerce. That said, M-PESA and mobile money do not equate to financial inclusion and won't, until new services are created, prices drop, and interoperability between mobile money players and banks is a seamless reality.

But if you think of the payment and transfer system as a transactional rail like a canal or a railroad, which opens up a range of unknown possibilities as entrepreneurs develop new products and services, then the expectation would be that mobile money will certainly lead to financial inclusion and more productive use of money – assuming the appropriate banking infrastructure is in place.

"The three factors of financial inclusion are proximity, trust and affordability," says Ignacio Mas. "Meeting these three factors requires a combination of scale and density of service. Retail is about location, banking is about trust, and infrastructure is about low unit costs. People need to transact as near as possible to their doorstep, in a totally secure way under the full protection of regulation and supervision and backed by a brand they trust. Providers need to avoid heavy local fixed costs (branches), which represent the main barrier to territorial expansion. This is where mobile money – and branchless banking more broadly – come in."

A study by the Bill & Melinda Gates Foundation identified 90 formal financial institutions that had integrated their operations with mobile money (primarily M-PESA) and found few providers who were not doing so. "Apart from turning a phone into a virtual ATM card, a basket of products is in the offing, with banks scrambling to ascend this very platform they so feared when it first came," says Mukhisa Kituyi, Director, The Kenya Institute of Governance.

Meanwhile, as more people use different types of financial services, they become more comfortable with basic banking principles and financial tools, which bodes well for future adoption. When ATMs were introduced in Kenya, people were initially hesitant to make the leap to trusting a machine on a wall with their money.

"When we rolled out ATMs there was this huge, massive effort that we undertook to educate and convince people to use those ATMs," says Matthew Krueger a member of the M-Banking Research & Strategy team at Equity Bank. "People would be staying in a queue at a banking hall and the ATM would be right outside and no one would be using it and some were just doing a withdrawal. So at the beginning we would have branch people go through the line and say – 'let me show you' – they go hand in hand to the ATM and demystify the use of ATM and demonstrate how people wouldn't lose their money."

One key fact about the poor and their money that has been observed through financial dairies over the last decade is that those living on $1 or $2 a day, who would appear to be of little or no value to a financial institution, actually have rather large cash flows. They are unpredictable, oscillating like an electric current, and often balance out at the end of a given term (day, week or month) at close to zero. Sometimes, the cash is converted into an asset, such as a cow or chicken, which is harder to subdivide or liquidate than hard cash. But in the interim, the volumes of cash are high, a factor of 10x or 20x above the long term average balance, and that should be of interest to a financial service provider – if it could figure out how to both handle millions of small transactions and price them accordingly.

NEW FINANCIAL PRODUCTS FOR THE UNBANKED

M-KESHO (see Chapter 3), the hybrid bank-telecom product jointly developed by Equity Bank and Safaricom, which was the first major new service to ride the M-PESA rails. It allows people with no history of banking to open a savings account at Equity Bank, and to use six months of M-PESA transaction records as a credit history source for taking out small loans. In roughly a year, M-KESHO attracted 1 million subscribers, although the vast majority of them were already Equity Bank account holders. In addition, while M-KESHO allows people to transfer money from the bank to M-PESA, there is a bank charge to transfer, and an M-PESA charge to withdraw. This double charge turns a potentially breakthrough product – one that could literally bank the previously unbanked – into a clunky product seemingly grafted together by two companies with deep suspicion of each other.

Equity Bank proceeded to launch other products with Safaricom's competitors, i.e. yuCash and Iko Pesa (Swahili equivalent for 'there is money'). These products link to a core bank account and are well positioned to bring the unbanked into mainstream banking. Equity's biggest play, however, may be its partnership with Orange Telecom to launch Orange Money; both the bank's and the telecom's agents will funnel customers to the fledgling service, as well as connect them to a fully fledged banking system.

JIPANGE KUSAVE (PLAN TO SAVE): LIQUIDITY AND SAVINGS

A newer and much more experimental product for saving and borrowing designed around M-PESA is *Jipange Kusave* ("plan to save"), offered by an independent third party (Mobile Ventures Kenya Ltd.), which is neither a bank nor a telecom. Jipange Kusave, which relies on M-PESA, is a savings and loan product that allows participants to save towards lump sums on an irregular schedule. The process starts with a small loan, a portion of which is kept back as savings for the customer.

The theory, developed by Stuart Rutherford (see Chapter 4) with microfinance institutions in Asia over a 20 year period, is that the poor need a flexible tool or service that fits their roller-coaster cash flow, and their constant hedging against risks and the temptation to spend. It's a product designed around liquidity (not interest on savings). Jipange Kusave, in fact, mirrors how many people need to borrow and try to save at the same time. It offers structure and process for managing liquidity through 'draw down' when credit is needed and a regular build up of funds in a 'remote' place that builds savings.

In short, Jipange Kusave is not a standard bank product aimed at the poor – but a new nonbank product designed especially for the needs of the poor. Because the amounts saved and borrowed are typically small, a commercial bank would not be able to profitably provide the service without charging high fees – but with M-PESA as the transactional rail it is possible to accommodate many very small transactions at friendlier terms. The hitch is that the Central Bank will only allow a licensed bank to offer the service, which has been deemed to be a deposit taker, so Mobile Ventures is still seeking a partner to launch the product commercially.

Even customers who already have a bank savings account appreciate Jipange Kusave because it protects their savings against withdrawal until the target is reached. Enforced illiquidity, which is a key element of ROSCAs and ASCAs, is as important for the poor as it is for the rich, who lock up money in long-term CDs and other quasi-liquid vehicles. Others appreciate the ability to take out a loan before they have even started saving.

TONE KWA TONE PATA PUMP (DROP BY DROP GETS THE PUMP): MOBILE LAYAWAY

A similar product, in that it sets a target and enforces illiquidity until the target is reached, comes from a product manufacturer. KickStart is an NGO whose mission is to identify profitable business opportunities open to thousands of very poor people; then design, manufacture and mass market simple moneymaking tools that unlock these business opportunities.

KickStart's best selling product is a metal, pedal-powered pump aptly named the Super MoneyMaker, which allows a single smallholder farmer working with a partner to irrigate up to two acres in eight hours – a 16-fold increase in efficiency over manual irrigation methods. The Super MoneyMaker, which simultaneously pumps and pushes water (up to 100 metres away), sells for roughly $105 – three months' wages for the average purchasing farmer. The smaller, more portable, manually operated Hip Pump, which alternates pull and push pumping, costs about $40.

Since it entered the Kenyan market in 1998, KickStart has sold over 64,500 pumps (and over 178,500 worldwide). KickStart's surveys, conducted two months and 18 months after purchase, document a dramatic impact. Purchasing households experience an average 1100% rise in farm income – from $100/yr. to $1100/yr. – and a 200-300% rise in HHI income, in the first year of pump ownership.

KickStart has faced two main impediments in selling its pumps. One is a lack of finance; the second is lack of access to a water source. Most smallholder farmers who lack access to a stream or pond can reach water by digging a 5 to 60 foot well. But in Kenya, as throughout most of Africa, less than 5% of farmers use such mechanical irrigation. As manual bucket-and-rope irrigation from ponds and streams requires two person days for each eighth of an acre, most farmers subsist by cultivating commodity crops fed by monsoon rains, such as maize. These crops yield low financial returns and are primarily stored to feed the household.

Early adopters of KickStart pumps, as with any technology, were better educated and more financially secure, and thus less risk averse. For many farmers, $40 or $105 is an unimaginable expenditure; for others, it seems possible and certainly desirable given the quick returns on investment, but difficult to come up with the money. So KickStart has leveraged M-PESA to design and develop a mobile layaway service: *Tone Kwa Tone Pata Pump* (Swahili for "Drop by Drop Gets the Pump").

Years ago, KickStart noticed that informal cash layaway was occurring, as many local agricultural retailers who had good relationships with farmers would set up layaway programmes. But not all farmers had good relationships with dealers, and without a high level of trust, cash-based layaway is limited.

With the formal layaway service, when a farmer makes a payment, he receives a confirmatory SMS from Safaricom, followed by one from KickStart. From KickStart's perspective, mobile money is cleaner for accountability than cash, which would require dealers to maintain records. Farmers like the system because they can make payments from home, saving themselves the time and money that a trip to the dealer would require. Farmers put down 15-18% of the total cost, depending on the product, and then have three months to complete payments (if they drop out of the programme, their money is refunded, minus a nonrefundable service fee and a cancellation fee of the same value). Payments can be any size above a minimum of KShs 100 shillings ($1.25).

Farmers use M-PESA's Pay Bill function to send mobile money to KickStart's "business number". Many have never before used Pay Bill, which is more heavily used in urban settings to pay utility bills, and initially there is some hesitation, but support from salespeople and the dual confirmation messages quickly encourage them to continue.

The 30 KShs transaction fee to send money through Pay Bill is split between KickStart and the farmer. "Some farmers have complained about it, but the way we explain it is: How much do you spend to get to town to the dealer shop? And how much to get home? They say something like 200 bob [English slang for shilling], and another 200 bob to get back. When you know you are saving 400 bob, spending 20 bob on a transaction fee makes sense," explains Charlene Chen, the Product Manager of Services at KickStart.

The primary alternative funding device, microloans, is problematic for most farmers. Their irregular income streams based on crop harvests don't lend themselves to regular monthly payments. And, of course, the interest rates charged are often high, which has led many farmers to default and forfeit collateral such as cows or land. Savings goals, as evidenced by Jipange Kusave, and targeted savings or asset financing, as evidenced by KickStart's mobile layaway service, are essentially a friendlier inverse of the typical microloan, except that you are paying in advance on your own schedule, rather than after the fact on the microfinance institution's schedule.

Having tested the programme with Safaricom, KickStart expects to engage other mobile money partners such as Airtel, which operates in Kenya and Tanzania, the two countries where most MoneyMaker pumps are sold. "We are really excited about the idea of partnering with mobile operators because if we can train their mobile money agents to market the service, then we can dramatically increase awareness," says Chen of KickStart.

PENSION AND MICROINSURANCE FOR THE POOR

Seven out of 10 in the "informal sector," which is where most Kenyans work as day labourers or artisans, have no retirement or pension plans. In recent years, a number of so-called "individual" pension plans have been designed, but a major problem for those who are unbanked has been the difficulty of making regular payments. From the perspective of the plan administrator, the huge administrative costs of accepting many small, irregular cash payments make such plans inefficient, even if profitable.

However, the ease of making mobile micropayments has revolutionized these individual plans. The Mbao Pension Scheme for jua kali, established in late 2010 by the Kenya National Jua Kali Cooperative Society (see Chapter 4), would not have been possible without mobile money, and the volume of small transactions it generates.

Orange Money, which was introduced in Kenya in 2010 and had fewer than 25,000 subscribers, entered a partnership with Telposta Pension Scheme to dispatch dues through Orange Money, instead of using the conventional banking services. Rather than travelling several kilometres to a commercial bank each month, members can visit one of 3,000 Equity Bank or Orange agents to withdraw cash, with the fee paid by Telposta Pension Scheme. Because the payment is distributed through a financial institution, the programme connects the poor to formal financial services.

M-Bima, a mobile-to-mobile, micro-insurance premium payment programme offered by Cooperative Insurance Company of Kenya Limited (CIC), has partnered with M-PESA, Yu-Cash, and Airtel Money, to allow customers to remit micropayments of KShs 20 (USD .25). Nelson Kuria, Managing Director of CIC, notes that the success of a micro-insurance product depends on whether it is "designed to accommodate the policyholder's irregular cash flows... and carries limited screening requirements that have kept customers away in the past."

Mothers and pregnant women who have no medical coverage are benefiting from two mobile money based products. Mamakiba (translating to 'Mother + Savings') and Changamka (translating to 'brighten up') were designed to help these women save in advance for upcoming expenses.

Mamakiba is an SMS based savings calculator and prepayment tracking tool that uses the same concept as KickStart's mobile layaway or Jipange Kusave – saving with a target in mind. The target in this case is clinical delivery. Mamakiba provides reminders of the total amount as well as the minimum needed to be deposited to the savings account before the next visit to the clinic. Every time a mother makes a deposit to her account, she receives an SMS confirmation indicating the amount sent, the new total savings and the remaining balance.

Changamka is another savings plan for pregnant women. It uses the Pay Bill function of M-PESA to enable them to push savings to a smart card, called the maternity card. The card enables the bearer to access antenatal, maternity and postnatal services at selected clinics and maternity facilities. The card is available at the participating health facilities at a cost of KShs 250 ($3.13) and can be topped up by M-PESA or at the hospital terminals. Mothers who use the card are entitled to a discount on listed prices depending on the programme they are signed up for.

VISION 2030 AND FINANCIAL INCLUSION

Kenya's development blueprint, Vision 2030 (published in 2008), seeks to elevate the country from a low to a medium income country by 2030, emulating the path of Asian tigers such as Malaysia and South Korea. It's certainly an ambitious goal for a country without vast natural resources beyond its wildlife, and presumes 25 years averaging 10% GDP growth! Only a few countries in world history have accomplished that, and they are all small and resource rich – Equatorial Guinea (1985-2004, 12% growth), Botswana (1966-1991, 13.1% growth) and Oman (1961-1986, 13.4% growth). China (9.9%), Singapore (9.5%) and Hong Kong (9.1%) – the latter two small islands (and thus outliers) – effectively hit 10% growth as well for a 25 year period. In 2010, Kenya's GDP increased by 5%, an improvement over the previous two years, when growth was neglible due to the post-election violence, but a far cry from the Asian tiger benchmark.

In addition to bolstering other sectors such as agriculture and manufacturing, Vision 2030 also calls for increasing access to formal financial services from current levels of 23% to more than 60% of the bankable (adult) population. Between 2006 and 2009, the last year measured, access increased from 18% to 23%, which many attribute to M-PESA. The ultimate goal is to increase savings and investments to 30% of GDP, in the hope of sparking more greenfield business development that attracts low-productivity workers from small farms.

This transformation will have to be achieved through mobile finance and branchless banking. According to CGAP's "Scenarios for Branchless Banking in 2020," for Kenya to reach middle income levels of branches and ATMs at current costs, it would require capital expenditure of some $2 billion – six times the pretax profit of the entire Kenyan banking sector in 2008.

While M-PESA and mobile money services in general may not provide sophisticated financial services beyond transfer, it's clear that they do provide access to a range of providers for previously excluded populations. And, based on the few but powerful new products that have been designed in the first few years of mobile money, it's safe to assume that increasingly powerful and targeted applications will provide more and more people with insurance, savings and loan capabilities, and investment options. Whether this takes Kenya from 23% to 60% with access to "formal financial services" may be moot. The meter is going in the right direction.

****

Mama Edna is a small-scale maize farmer who also sells fruit and vegetables in a kiosk in Sotik, a town about 260 kms West of Nairobi. When Victor, a sales representative for KickStart, approached her one evening at her kiosk with a plan to buy a pump, she was sold on the idea at once. But she was hesitant to make a deal because she also had to pay school fees for her children. When Victor fully explained the Tone kwa Tone Pata Pump service, she felt better and asked Victor to give her the night to think over the whole idea.

Victor showed up in her homestead the next day, and Mama happily registered. An SMS from Kickstart confirmed her registration; she was on her way to getting a Super Money Maker pump. Over the next few months, Mama made multiple deposits to the Pay Bill number Victor had given her. She was able to track her progress on payments via SMS's sent from the company. "Mama Edna, as of the end of February, you have paid KShs 2450 (14%) in total towards your Super Money Maker pump. Your remaining balance is KShs. 6050. ASANTE!" For every payment she made, she received a confirmation from M-PESA and from KickStart. The transparent communication was encouraging. "The best thing about it is that you only deposit as much as you have and the messages sent on each deposit will guide you," she says. A transaction fee of KShs 25 is charged with each payment.

When she got a congratulatory SMS message from KickStart – "Congratulations Edna, we have received your final Tone kwa tone payment. Victor Agisa will make sure your Super Money Maker pump is available in one week"--she found it hard to believe that she had completed her payments. The fact that she also saw Victor's name on the SMS assured her that this was no conman scheme, as she had been warned by her friends. She was finally going to get her pump. And she was very determined to make money with it.

A few days later, Victor drove into her homestead and took Mama to the Kenya Farmers' Association shop in town, where she picked up her pump. Her farmhand already had ideas on how this amazing tool was going to generate income beyond farming. In the nearby river, the young man planned to start a car wash business where he would charge KShs 100 for every car. He now does this every day after completing his farm chores. On the first day Mama

Edna got KShs 300 from the business. She also made plans to move beyond just maize and start growing her own fruit and vegetables. She sees a future business where she will be able to supply food to schools and hospitals in the area.

The young farm hand is equally enthusiastic about the new machine. "Kama siyo hii ningekwama" ["if it weren't for this I'd be stuck"] was his first reaction. He can now fetch water for the cattle easily, as well as keep his car washing business going. His wages have increased and the relationship with his employer is better.

Mama Edna feels that most people would like to acquire goods through such a layaway service – she considers bank loans a liability. She doesn't like paying interest, and would rather save up and pay in advance as she did with her pump. "I am now the envy of the village, thanks to the amazing Super Money Maker."

Chapter 6
SWAHILI SILICON VALLEY

"Safaricom is an innovative company. We came up with sambaza, to share minutes with others. We came up with "please call me," to 'flash' people without using up minutes. We came up with various innovative low-cost, low-denomination scratch cards and the one with emergency credit, where you send an SMS and you get 50 bob credit – Okoa Jahazi.

"How did we innovate? We had a department of innovation, which encouraged free thinking. People could come up with any whacky idea, it didn't matter. And we had a process called the gate process, where a committee made a decision – 'ok that is too whacky,' 'proceed with this lot' or 'go do some more work on this lot and then come back.' And we had a process for taking new products through a quick cycle of six months gestation period or less. But in the end, only one person made the decision. And that was me. And that is how you innovate. You cannot innovate by committee. Because there's always someone on the committee who will slow things down. In the end, if you want to innovate, you need to have a single decision maker."

Michael Joseph, former CEO, Safaricom, interview with the authors, June 2011

****

M-PESA started as an add-on service that might improve financial inclusion and also stop customer churn away from Safaricom to lower priced competitors. But it's no longer a mere service. M-PESA has morphed into a fully fledged platform, much like the iPhone, and has spawned a whole new ecosystem of add-on services.

M-PESA is at the centre of an economic vortex, much as the personal computer in the 1980s, the Internet in the 1990s, and the iPhone in the 2000s were, in developed economies. In the U.S., Google and Microsoft engineers eventually filter into the broader ecosystem; in Kenya, M-PESA engineers are behind some of the most promising startups. Companies with names like Symbiotic, Tangazoletu, Webtribe, Zege Technologies, Mobile Commerce Ventures, MTL Systems, Coretec Systems and Solutions, Verviant Consulting, Flexus Technologies, Intrepid, Kopo Kopo – and products with names like iPay, PesaPal, Moco, Spotcash, Jambopay, M-Payer, crowdpesa. This could be Silicon Valley, Swahili style!

iHub in Nairobi hosts "pitch events," linking startups to venture capitalists, much like Guy Kawasaki's Garage.com in the U.S. in the go-go 1990's, when entrepreneurs would give a 30 second "elevator pitch" to VCs. Agosta Liko, CEO of PesaPal, a tool for online merchants, refers to a "new commerce," the integration of internet and mobile channels to build a larger, more inclusive payments ecosystem. Danson Muchemi, CEO of JamboPay, says his service aims to mitigate the same market failure that gave rise to PayPal in the West, the need for secure and multi-channel access to e-commerce. Philip Nyamwaya, CEO of iPay, says, "We've come up with Kenyan solutions for Kenya, for the region, for the continent."

The prevalence of the word "pay" in company names attests to the focus on payments. Money is moving in Kenya. Imagine this: PewaHewa.com is powered by iPay, both Kenyan companies – one selling music *a la carte* like iTunes, the other facilitating payments via multiple mobile money platforms.

If one ripple effect from M-PESA is distributing e-money and cash deeper into remote villages and boosting farm incomes and employment, the other is the diametric opposite – sparking a high-tech explosion in Nairobi that many cities around the world would like to see in their backyard. This fast developing ecosystem has spawned many Kenyan greenfield companies, as well as venture– backed companies from the U.S. who have set up East African headquarters in Nairobi – a city that five years ago was wracked by horrific ethnic and inter-tribe post-election violence. Global players such as Google, MasterCard, Facebook, Visa and Nokia are on the ground with offices and well entrenched in the ecosystem.

"There are a ton of small entrepreneurs working in mobile money and they are arriving from four vastly different directions," says Mark Pickens, formerly a microfinance specialist at the Consultative Group to Assist the Poor (CGAP), which is part of the World Bank. "One is adjacent industries, such as m-health. Another is third party mobile software developers, feeding off the action. Then there are the classic tech entrepreneurs, kind of Silicon Valley meets Rift Valley. Finally, the financial services sector."

Mobile money has sparked two broad areas of enterprise innovation. First, a whole new class of company is using M-PESA's payment functionality (including Bill Pay and Bulk Payments) as the core of its business model and consumer proposition. The efficiency gains of switching from cash to e-money payments make these businesses profitable or, in the case of non-profits, more sustainable and thus more attractive to funders.

Another class of greenfield companies connects mobile money providers to the internet to facilitate payments and shopping. In a country where broadband internet is limited in many areas and has achieved relatively low, single-digit rates of penetration, many of the "new commerce" solutions are essentially creating the mobile internet. Some of these companies, such as Cellulant and Craft Silicon, both of which are Nairobi-based companies that operate in multiple countries, started operations before M-PESA, but are now dedicated to mobile money applications. Other companies connect M-PESA to back office accounting systems, which is key to streamlining businesses and speeding up the notification of payments.

THE "MOBILE" BUSINESS MODEL

Mobile payments certainly improve efficiencies for businesses that have operated on cash for years, as we saw in Chapter 5. But starting from scratch with mobile is clearly more effective than converting midstream, because it's so hard to disconnect from expensive legacy systems. Beyond that, the ability to offer mobile payments is an incentive to conceive of new approaches to old businesses, such as education or microfinance, and hopefully improve on them. In many other cases, particularly those that offer social or public goods, which might typically be a government purview, mobile payments allow delivery of goods that was not possible before because of the difficulty of collecting micropayments.

Cashless Microfinance

Musoni is the world's first 100% mobile powered, cashless, microfinance institution (MFI). All loans are disbursed to a mobile phone; all loans are repaid via

M-PESA, with future plans to connect to the other mobile money providers. When clients are in arrears, they receive an SMS notification. While cashless, Musoni is not branchless – believing that customers, especially those at the base of the pyramid, need human interaction to feel comfortable with borrowing.

Musoni (m for mobile, *usoni* for future) adheres to the Grameen Bank group-lending concept, targeting the poor who are expected to meet in groups. But the ability to pay up front when cash is on hand obviates the need to store money or carry it to a meeting. It also frees up time at the meeting to discuss financial matters, rather than merely collecting cash.

Compared to traditional MFIs, Musoni has a significant competitive advantage because it operates so much more efficiently. Most importantly, the effective annual interest rate (although most loans are repaid with a month or two) is 11-12%, lower than the typical 20% to 80% that most MFIs charge. In addition, loan processing is very fast.

"For security purposes, we normally tell our customers that they will get their money 72 hours after making an application," says George Maina, Musoni's CEO in Nairobi. "This is still better than anybody else in the market. But we always want to surprise them, so within 24 hours, they actually get their money. Compare that to the conventional MFI, where you have to come to the office, take the cheque to the bank, and wait for four days for it to clear." Of the KShs 30 transaction fee, Musoni absorbs KShs 10, as an incentive to enlist new customers.

Operated by a Dutch holding company, Musoni's back office is based in Holland, which the company claims is more efficient and allows a better jumping off point for entry into new countries. Loan applications and processing are sent from Kenya to Holland for approval; all disbursements and payments are tracked in real time in both Kenya and Holland. With no need for a pool of data-entry clerks, staffing needs are minimal. When a client repays a loan from his or her phone, the number serves as an account number; the client notes "lr" for loan repayment. If a friend or relative is helping to repay, he or she notes "si" for stand-in, then inserts the phone number of the actual client.

In its first year, Musoni opened two branches in Nairobi, and in its second year expanded to Thika, a market town about an hour north. In addition to further expansion in Kenya, the company is looking to move into other countries, where it will encounter a wider range of mobile money payment systems. And it is applying to the Central Bank for a deposit-taking licence. "If you are telling clients that they can save from wherever, people will be encouraged to save," says Maina.

Cashless Schools

Bridge International Academies is doing in education what Musoni is doing in microfinance – starting from scratch with a cashless, mobile payments system. With funding from Pearson and Omidyar Network, Bridge is a K-4, for-profit "school-in-a-box" franchise model targeting parents in the slums of Nairobi and other poor areas in Kenya.

Started in 2009, Bridge accepts payments only through M-PESA or direct deposits into its Equity Bank account. This reduces the logistical problems of handling cash and collections, and simplifies payments to teachers and suppliers. Record keeping is enhanced, although Bridge, like many other Pay Bill clients, would like to find a way to better integrate M-PESA records with its own accounting software. "Everything we do is about efficiency," says founder Jay Kimmelman, an American educational software entrepreneur who started the business with his wife, Shannon May. "We need to choose systems that allow us to be efficient, transparent and accountable. Being cashless enables us to achieve that."

"Let's says a school manager wants to buy water from a local vendor. The manager sends an SMS to our system requesting payment of KShs 2000 for water to John Njenga. Our system automatically determines whether the request is from an authorized person, whether John Njenga is a pre-approved water vendor, and whether the amount is within the school's budget. If approved, payment is automatically sent. The school manager (principal) has the ability to manage expenses, but they are centrally approved and audited." Teachers, of course, are paid by M-PESA, which means they don't have to worry about walking home with a wad of cash on payday, a problem in many schools.

Bridge built 10 schools in its first year, and expects to build another 50 over the next few years. "In four or five years, we aim to open one new school per day. This enterprise is built on scalability," says Kimmelman. "The idea is to move into other African countries, such as Ghana, Uganda, and Nigeria, as well as India."

Bridge builds schools in densely populated areas after extensive research into land availability and demographics. Most students (90%) live within 500 metres of school, and pay less than $4 a month. Schools go up in five months, at a cost of about $1,800 per classroom. There is no electricity, and a latrine rather than lavatory. "We have real-time information about which students have paid and should be in school – but we don't even have electricity in the schools," says Kimmelman. Students pay a small fee for lunches cooked by people in the local community. All lessons are totally scripted, minute by minute, from 7:30 to 5 every day. This allows beginning teachers, following an eight week training course, to focus on teaching – and administrators to more easily evaluate them. Both teachers and managers are evaluated on a weekly business.

The one aspect of M-PESA that Kimmelman does not like is the transaction fee. "Parents pay KShs 320 per month, in addition to a KShs 20 fee, or roughly 8%. So that is significant. We think as competition comes to the market those fees are going to start declining. We are working in communities with some of the poorest families in the country, and the incremental fees are taken seriously. That's why we also let parents deposit in a bank, for free."

The radical franchise and electronic payments business model appears to be working; in two years, more than 3,500 students have enrolled. When cash is removed from the system and replaced by technology, fast scaling is possible, even in a business driven by human interaction.

Maji ya Compiuta

Access to clean drinking water is an ongoing challenge in rural Kenya. (In 2011, northern Kenya, bordering Somalia, was suffering its worst drought in 60 years.) In the semi-arid, rural town of Katitika, for example, it's so dry that even some cacti don't survive long droughts. But a joint project, between Safaricom and Denmark's Grundfos Lifelink, a global water pump manufacturer, allows villagers to buy water with micropayments from a community water pump. Villagers transfer M-PESA to a smart card ("key bobs") that can be used to draw water from specially calibrated, solar powered water pumps.

This *maji ya compiuta* (computer water) opens a whole world of possibilities throughout Kenya. Because attendants are not necessary to monitor water use (which limits hours, increases costs and invites fraud), and because payments are transparent and instantly recorded, the system can be easily maintained and monitored by local communities. In case of pump malfunction, an alarm carried by the Safaricom network sounds in Grundfos's regional office. Water remittances through M-PESA encourage private investors to enter rural areas they previously would have bypassed. Grundfos Lifelink is looking to deploy 10 such solar pumps in different communities. In Katitika, the community is essentially buying the water pump on credit at an affordable rate through its utility fees.

Before maji ya compiuta, a hand pump that rarely worked had been used. Alternatively, villagers walked 90 minutes to a river and carried water home. The new, high-tech solar pump, along with a 10,000 litre tank, ensures a steady supply of nearby water. Villagers save time and money, and have even used the water to start businesses such as brick making, kitchen gardens and tree nurseries – more than 20 gardens have been planted since the water project started in 2009, according to the Iris Center's (University of Maryland) study of community level effects. The water is attracting people from other villages, so the community is selling bottled water by jerry can. One member of the water committee commented, "We can even go down to two shillings and still pay our loan and bring money into the community because the demand is there."

Grundfos Lifelink has a similar project in the village of Kami ya Juu, north of Mt. Kenya, 285 kilometres from Nairobi. Ten years ago, the government chose to restrict water to the larger town of Isiolo, and cut off water to Kami ya Juu and other smaller villages. Villagers were left to fetch water from the bush, walking hours to do so. Even then, they had to boil the water or risk disease such as cholera. "The water isn't clean," says village resident Ann Akopi. "The people who live up the hill wash both themselves and their clothes in the brook."

Tension over lack of water between pastoral and agricultural tribes led to a spate of ethnic clashes in 2009, leaving a large population of internally displaced people in Kami ya Juu. Kenya Red Cross, targeting access to water as the source of conflict, reached out to Grundfos. As in Katitika, Grundfos installed a solar-powered water pump, combined with payments via mobile phone organized by a microfinance organisation. Twenty litres of water costs KShs 2 With assistance from the Danish Red Cross, employees of Grundfos donated the pump and its installation. The Grundfos maji ya compiuta would not be possible without M-PESA remittances, which are delivering money on a regular basis into rural and remote towns and villages.

In 2011, as 3.5 million Kenyans faced starvation due to drought (and thousands of Somali refugees flooded into the country), Kenya Red Cross engaged Safaricom and other corporate and mobile operators to quickly raise money for famine relief. Safaricom set up a special M-PESA Pay Bill number, while KCB set up a special bank account for donations. Other mobile operators also joined with their mobile money services. Kenyans for Kenya hoped to raise KShs 500 million in four weeks, but did it in half the time. The majority of payments were a minimal KShs 10, according to Betty Mwangi of Safaricom. In a fund-raising appeal earlier in the year, without mobile money and micropayments as an option, the Red Cross fell 80% short of its target.

Kilimo Salama (Safe Farming) Crop Insurance

A new mobile money insurance programme generates even higher sales of seeds as it protects farmers. *Kilimo Salama* ("safe farming") provides protection against crop losses due to drought or too much rain, as measured by 30 automated weather stations. Since many farmers are hesitant to invest in superior seeds, fertilizers or herbicides for fear of crop losses, especially in the first year or two after a disaster, this programme encourages them to buy better seeds for a 5% insurance premium, and get their money back if the crop fails in part or full. The administrators of the programme – UAP Insurance of Kenya, Safaricom, and Syngenta Foundation for Sustainable Agriculture – match the farmers' 5% investment, according to a report in *The Economist* .

When farmers purchase seeds, agro retailers use a phone camera to scan the bar code, which generates a confirmatory SMS to the farmer. Data from the nearest weather station is sent to the insurer, where experts determine whether the crops will reach fruition. No insurance adjusters need to visit the farms, as all data is sent electronically. If the answer is no, payments are sent directly to farmers via M-PESA. These three-cornered electronic feeds reduce transaction costs and make the programme viable. During the pilot programme, farmers doubled the amount of seeds under insurance.

Kilimo Salama was launched after a pilot where several hundred maize farmers insured their farm inputs during the long rainy season. After a crippling drought, farmers were compensated according to the severity of the drought as measured at their weather station (a 30 percent and 80 percent payout, respectively). Kilimo Salama features many elements – like the mobile phone registry and payment system and distribution through rural retailers – that are micro-insurance firsts.

THE "NEW COMMERCE" PLAYERS

Hundreds of Kenyan businesses are now integrated with M-PESA and other mobile money services, according to a survey conducted by the Bill & Melinda Gates Foundation. And since few of these companies have their own software engineers to integrate mobile money with their own back office systems, a veritable army of young wizards has emerged or arrived in Nairobi to do the dirty work of patching together multiple financial and corporate systems with multiple mobile money systems.

One of the more established mobile systems companies is Cellulant, a Nairobi based company that started in 2004, and now operates in nine African countries. Cellulant was co-founded by Ken Njoroge, who cut his teeth at a Nairobi digital ad agency, 3Mice. Initially, the company was set up to sell music via mobile downloads, but, with the surge of M-PESA, shifted to help banks integrate with mobile money systems.

Cellulant's first product was Commerce 360, which allows users to create a mobile wallet to connect to banks, and make payments to utilities and cable TV (DSTV). An enhancement to Commerce 360, Lipuka, allows customers' payments across multiple wallets, plus realtime settlements. (In most cases, M-PESA payments processed by Pay Bill are batched together and often take 24-48 hours to clear.) For example, when you pay Multichoice for DSTV via M-PESA, you don't have to call Multichoice to be reconnected, as you once did, nor does Multichoice have to manually record your payment in its accounting system.

Another "new commerce" player is Craft Silicon, started in 2000 by Kamal Budhabhatti, an Indian immigrant. The company's bread and butter is developing core banking systems, microfinance systems, and e-payments switches for large banks in 40 countries, including India, Nigeria and Tanzania. Today, Craft is piloting Elma, an "end-to-end e-commerce over mobile" solution that is web-based, but delivered through mobile phones. For a subscription fee of $1 per month, users can pay any bills, transfer money, select seats at events (such as movies), buy and sell stocks, and view traffic cameras. The value proposition is that transaction fees are reduced to nil ($1/month). "Kenyans need much more than money transfer," says Budhabhatti. "And they need a product that is independent of the mobile service provider."

Numerous other firms are dedicated to integrating mobile money and back office systems for small MFIs. As more MFIs distribute loans and receive repayments via mobile money, they encounter difficulties reconciling accounts. In 2007, when M-PESA was in pilot with Faulu, it was the vast disconnect between e-payments and manual data recordkeeping that caused the mismatch. Today, of course, most MFIs use computerized recordkeeping, but still have to manually download mobile payments, reconcile them and then upload to their database. The process is slow, expensive and error prone.

"With technology such as cloud computing, savings groups such as SACCOs can now cut their operation costs by trimming the number of their field officers, as well as reducing fraud," says Oscar Ahere, a product development manager at Flexus Technologies. The company's web-based application, Kopesha, automates processes that have long been manual, such as processing loan applications and disbursing loans. Annual licence fees for the cloud-based service are about a quarter of software fees. Flexus Technologies is a Kenyan company that partnered with PayG Solutions from the U.K. (several PayG programmers worked on the initial M-PESA software).

Kopo Kopo is a U.S. based Company with East African headquarters at the m:lab incubator in Nairobi, with seed capital investments from the U.S. (Gray Ghost Ventures and Presumed Abundance), Kopo Kopo builds software-as-a-service (SAAS) platforms to integrate mobile money systems with a range of back office systems used by MFIs and SACCOs, who lease the software for $400 or less per month. Contrast that with paying anywhere from 5 to 10 employees from $20,000 to $50,000 a year.

NAIROBI'S SWAHILI SILICON VALLEY

The rapid spread of mobile telephony starting in 2000, followed by the rapid spread of mobile money starting in 2007, has clearly spawned a new ICT (Information, and Communications Technology) cluster in Nairobi. It started with electronics shops selling and repairing phones, morphed into software developers working on their own to develop apps to build a better platform, and now has the full support of the Kenyan government as it looks to foster IT as a pillar for future economic growth. The government, with support from the International Finance Corporation (IFC) of the World Bank, is constructing a sprawling 5,000 acre technology park (Malili Technology Park) to promote BPO (business process outsourcing) as well as content and app development. "The ICT revolution is starting to connect to other sectors and starting to influence the old economy and causing an enormous amount of growth," says Wolfgang Fengler, lead economist at the Nairobi office of the World Bank.

A key focal point for new startups is iHub ("innovation" Hub) in Nairobi, co-founded by Eric Hersman, also the co-founder of Ushahidi. Ushahidi is not connected to the mobile money craze, but is an ingenious open-source mobile application that has spread around the world. Ushahidi, which means "witness" in Swahili, is the Kenya based crowd-sourcing platform developed to track violence during and after the 2007-08 post-election violence in Nairobi through SMS. Ushahidi messages describe a basic situation, along with GPS coordinates. It has since been adapted for other emergency disaster situations, such as the 2010 earthquake in Haiti.

In 2010, with $2 million in funding from the Omidyar Network, Hersman co-founded iHub as a Nairobi incubator for high-tech startups. The modern work environment has an open layout with the look and feel of Silicon Valley – open spaces with plush couches and meeting areas for techies and investors.

iHub cross fertilizes with some major global firms, such as its partners Google, Nokia and Microsoft, which are learning how to adapt products for nonWestern cultures. In 2009, Google launched its G-Africa initiative to encourage software development in sub-Saharan Africa, and in 2010 Google started testing *Baraza* ("meeting place" in Swahili), a knowledge-sharing centre for East and Central Africans. Google Africa has also partnered with Wikipedia to create more Kiswahili content, done a great deal of work translating their popular Gmail service into local languages, and begun to map Africa's roads beyond the cities. According to Hersman, who is also author of the widely popular WhiteAfrican blog, Google Africa represents perhaps the best example of a global firm localizing content by cross-breeding its international technology expertise with local hires, interns and volunteers.

In its first year, iHub attracted more than 3,000 members, and spawned 12 companies. In 2011, iHub, partnering with the University of Nairobi and WWW Foundation, started m:Lab, focused specifically on mobile apps. Whive is a social media platform for Africa that operates in multiple languages, including tribal dialects. Zege Technologies automates the process of frequent payments through mobile money, with direct integration into enterprise level systems to avoid error prone manual reconciliation. And M-Farm provides an SMS-based application that connects farmers to provide buying and selling power, as well as providing weather and agricultural data. Seven companies were accepted for m:Lab. In addition to Kenyans, m:Lab attracted applicants from Rwanda and Uganda, indicating the growing allure of Nairobi as a technology hub for mobile developers in Africa.

"There is a paradigm shift. The PC users in the West do not understand the users of the mobile web in Africa. So it takes an entrepreneur from Africa to answer some of those hard questions," says Hersman, who, in addition to the WhiteAfrican blog, also operates the AfriGadget blog that touts local innovations. "It's a challenge to understand the needs of a culture that you don't share and then create a product for it. This is why so many of the platforms and products designed in the West fail in Africa. It's not that they're not well designed; they're just not designed by people who truly understand the needs of the customers in Africa. It's why rugged and efficient seed-planting devices will be created in rural Ghana. It's why Ushahidi and M-PESA had to come from a place like Kenya."

iHub has been instrumental in connecting entrepreneurs to venture capitalists, through "pitch events" where entrepreneurs are grilled by VCs. While Hersman notes that some "investors have connected with investees," iHub is still more of a pre-incubator for ideas than an incubator to lift ideas off the ground. In addition, the investor ecosystem is still quite thin, at least by Western standards, and deals are scarce.

"There's a growing community of VC firms, mostly foreign, some angel investors, mostly Kenyan, and an incredibly, vibrant tradition of investment clubs (chamas) which by one count have $470 million in assets in Kenya. But no one is investing in tech startups," says CGAP's Pickens. "VCs are looking to invest a minimum of $150,000, which is too much for most startups, and local angel investors prefer to see tangible assets that can be sold off. The chamas, though widespread, tend to invest in the stock market and more traditional businesses. As a result, the runway is very short, far shorter than the window of opportunity in Silicon Valley. Kenyan entrepreneurs have maybe a few months, or half a year. It's tough to iterate an idea and get the right recipe in such a short time."

Craft Silicon's Budhabhatti feels that the Kenyan IT community is innovative, but needs more business acumen to attract investment. "We do not follow the blue ocean strategy; we are all in the red ocean, chasing M-PESA. There is a lot of innovation, but all in the same direction. "

"I think the question we need to ask is, Why would investors want to invest in Kenya? Just because we are innovative? Just because there is an opportunity? There are opportunities in other countries as well. The government is spending on IT, but it's going to foreign multinationals, like Siemens, not local startups. Talent is not being utilized. If we want to scale, the country needs to change policies."

That's true, as it is in many parts of the world, including parts of the U.S. But the other way to look at Kenya's emerging IT hub is the short amount of time it's taken to build a fertile framework for ideas and business creation in a country that was wracked by violence five years ago, and that a decade ago had very few phones and a calcified banking system that catered exclusively to the rich. "What I find interesting is seeing Kenya as a place that doesn't import innovation but exports innovation," says the World Bank's Wolfgang Fengler. "Kenya shows the world innovation. That's quite unique."

Even Budhabhatti agrees. "Luckily, because M-PESA has made Kenya popular, we are now getting some deals in European countries. I even did a presentation in Papua New Guinea, and they said, 'You come from Kenya? You have all this mobile experience, good! And we signed a deal."

Says World Bank's Fengler: "The revolution has only started. Now that almost everyone in Kenya has a phone (increasingly connected to the internet), many more innovations will emerge – think Ushahidi – because information is the hardest currency in the 21st century and is now available to everyone at low cost."

****

"Nairobi is like San Francisco in 1993." Steve Landman, an investor from Southern California who flew in prior to the Pivot25 Mobile Apps and Developers Conference and Competition, said this about the Nairobi tech scene after his brief visit last month. Steve is no amateur when it comes to tech innovation.

He is a seasoned entrepreneur with several decades of experience in the tech scene, having founded and sold several companies, including two IPO's. Steve isn't alone in this opinion; people are starting to take notice of Nairobi, and for good reason.

Pivot25, held at the Ole Sereni Hotel in Nairobi in June, combined with the m:lab East Africa launch the following day, marked the dawn of a new era in the Nairobi tech scene.

We are walking boldly onto the international stage, and people are listening to what we have to say. We are proving to the world that East Africa is the place where the world's top investors come to unearth the next generation of big name players in the tech world.

Just 15 months after its inception, iHub Nairobi has surpassed 4,000 members and spawned the m:lab East Africa, a first of its kind mobile tech incubator located just a floor below the iHub in the Bishop Magua Centre. Only two years ago, no one would have believed that these dreams would become realities.

But they are, and it's no coincidence. Nairobi is filled with world class developers, coders, designers, programmers, creatives, researchers and entrepreneurs. We're just now starting to see all this potential enter into the spotlight to be magnified, harnessed and invested in.

While what has already happened here in Nairobi is certainly a great achievement, the future is what we should really be getting excited about. It's becoming increasingly obvious that this is only the tip of the iceberg. The vortex of entrepreneurship, innovation and value-creation is just starting to spin.

The spotlight is slowly beginning to shine on a new continent – our continent. However, just because the world is coming to us and the focus is shifting, doesn't mean we can't miss it.

A lot happened in San Francisco in the 18 years that passed from 1993 to 2011. A lot of hard work, key conversations, dynamic partnerships and strategic investments went into creating the cultural hotbed of entrepreneurship that it is today. That work is exactly what lies ahead of us, and it won't be easy. However, if we succeed, the returns will be exponential. The impact could change the face of East Africa as we know it.

What if we were the next example, rather than San Francisco? What if we were the comparison? What if people in the future could excitedly claim that their country was like Nairobi in 2011?

Ryan Delk, business development expert at iHub Nairobi, opinion piece in *Business Daily* (Kenya), August 9th 2011

Chapter 7
CHANGE IS NOT EASY

Ladies and Gentlemen:

The Government recognizes the vital role the financial system plays in the economy. This recognition is entrenched in the country's development blue print – Vision 2030, which aims at transforming the country into a newly industrialized middle-income country that provides high quality of life to its citizenry by the year 2030.

Vision 2030 envisages a financial sector that is vibrant and globally competitive in driving high levels of savings and financing the country's investment needs. To achieve this goal, however, three core objectives – enhancing financial stability, improving its efficiency, and expanding financial access – must be addressed. The financial sector has to collect savings from micro-savers and provide them to the real sector for productive investments.

Secure and high quality savings, affordable insurance services and pension schemes are financial services demanded by all, including poor households, who have suffered the most in terms of accessing these services. Poor households, the majority of whom are still unbanked, need to manage their finances efficiently through accessible and affordable financial services and reduce their vulnerability to fluctuations in cash flow, save for consumption smoothing, cope with emergencies like poor health and/or death and accumulate high quality savings for investment in household and other productive ventures. Considerable scope, therefore, exists for expanding access to financial services to the unbanked segments and markets in our economy.

The phenomenal success of mobile phone money transfers has put Kenya at the centre stage globally in terms of financial inclusion and innovation. But sustaining success has its challenges. We have to be ready to modify our businesses to cope and formulate rules to contain the main actors and new entrants to the business.

Njuguna Ndung'u, Governor, Central Bank of Kenya

****

As the mobile money market expands and evolves, Kenyan policymakers have choices to make. The big question: how can Kenya maintain the high level of mobile money innovation while increasing the level of competition to lower consumer prices? If the competition to Safaricom weakens or evaporates (in 2011 there were rumours that Essar was ready to sell its Yu business) prices are likely to remain where they are – far cheaper than money transfer costs five years ago, but still a significant barrier to the creation of a cashless society and the promise of greater financial inclusion. Unless someone can provide competition on the mobile money and money transfer front, there's no incentive for Safaricom to reduce transaction fees.

There are two main policy questions driving debate today. For mobile operators, the issue is interoperability between mobile money providers. For banks, the issue is levelling the playing field with regulations for cash merchants and bank agents.

INTEROPERABILITY BETWEEN MOBILE MONEY SERVICES

Most mobile money operators seek to establish themselves on a standalone basis and see interconnecting with other operators as a longer term issue. Early movers do not see much benefit in sharing their hard work with laggards, nor do they relish the complexity of negotiating with their competitors. However, a lack of interconnection can easily make it that much harder for mobile money services to scale fast. This, of course, was not the case with M-PESA, but you could argue that even in Kenya mobile money would be significantly more pervasive and effective if services were interoperable.

Bharti Airtel, among others, is demanding interoperability between mobile money systems. Many Kenyans carry multiple SIMs, and switch them in and out of their phone (or carry a dual SIM phone), depending on whether they are calling or transferring money. Connecting mobile money systems would expand the market for all players, who would then compete on services and prices, rather than control of the channel. Multiple SIMs and number portability are really no good for any carrier. "Multiple SIM cards are the enemy if you believe that the main reason why you are doing mobile money is to entangle your customers with a sticky service," says consultant Mas. "Churn will not be reduced if the customer selects which SIM card to use each time they want to do a transaction based on which mobile money network the recipient of the funds is on."

As an example, consider Tanzania, which has a 50% mobile phone penetration, and the largest player has a 40 percent market share. Assuming optimistically that this dominant mobile operator converts 50 percent of its customer base to mobile money, this represents a payment ecosystem touching just 10 percent of the population (50% x 40% x 50%). That is simply not enough to create a compelling proposition to users, and most likely not enough transaction volume to create a viable business case for a sufficiently large number of cash merchants. Even this dominant operator might be better off interconnecting with the mobile money and branchless banking schemes of other telecoms and banks. Yet this is not happening anywhere in the world, as both telecoms and banks want to go it alone, despite the fact that their efforts are going to be subscale.

Kenyans can send money from one mobile money network to another, but at a cost. M-PESA subscribers, for example, can send money to Bharti Airtel subscribers, but the Airtel recipient has to withdraw from an M-PESA agent and pay a surcharge (often twice the cost of an M-PESA charge). In addition, the recipient cannot send on the e-money, but can only cash out. The same is true in reverse.

Network operators argue in a letter sent to the Prime Minister that inter-network transfers are currently too expensive and that a central clearing house would lower the costs – and make it easier for Safaricom customers to switch to an alternative mobile network. They feel they should be allowed to connect to the M-PESA network – allowing their customers to send and receive money from M-PESA users – just as subscribers to different operators can make phone calls to each other. If the regulators (CCK) set interconnection fees for voice calls, why can't it set interconnection fees for access to the M-PESA network?

A *Business Daily* news report (June 14, 2011) spells out the issue:

"The clamour for a common mobile money transfer system follows a request by Airtel in February to have a seamless withdrawal mobile money transfer service, but the market leader Safaricom said this was likely to kill innovation in the money transfer industry as subscribers may not receive money sent to them instantly. Currently, recipients of money across networks receive an SMS notifying them that money has been sent to them and then use the message to withdraw from an agent of the transmitting operator. A task force set up by the Prime Minister's office has recommended that mobile firms should create a seamless mobile money transfer system regulated by Central Bank of Kenya."

Mr Mwaura Nduati, head of the national payments system at the Central Bank of Kenya and also a member of 12 member team that formed the task force, said CBK would not force any of the mobile firm's operators to share its mobile money network agents. "What we are asking of the mobile phone operators is similar to the banks' settlement payment system," said Mr. Nduati. "A central clearing house for mobile phone payments is likely to increase usage of the service just like sharing of ATMs by banks has increased uptake of debit cards."

Rosemary Atieno, a senior research fellow at the University of Nairobi, notes: "It is important to underline that M-PESA has a monopoly of the delivery channel, handling more than 80% of electronic money transactions in Kenya, hence has the ability to block access by imposing an interchange fee. This means that new electronic financial solutions may not be able to find competitive linkages, that is, whether and how they will integrate with Safaricom customers."

The problem is that Safaricom controls the SIM, and thus the channel, and can turn that off and on or charge what it feels the market will bear. Even banks want access to the SIM. "If we're going to provide mobile services for customers, we need access to the SIM card," says John Staley, head of mobile money for Equity Bank. "Whoever controls the SIM card, controls the ecosystem in Kenya." As it is, Equity Bank, which has offered mobile access to bank accounts since 2003 through its Eazzy 24/7, is reliant on USSD technology, which is slower and less reliable than STK (SIM Toolkit) technology. With Safaricom controlling the SIM, there was no way Eazzy 24/7 SMS Banking was going to compete with M-PESA.

Similarly, third party providers like Craft Silicon are finding mobile operators difficult to deal with. "The only way we can provide solutions to the base of the pyramid is putting our system on the SIM, or go with a USSD model where it will work on all the phones," says Kamal Budhabhatti, CEO of Craft Silicon, whose Elma payment product is operator agnostic. "USSD is so expensive. Putting it on the SIM, they won't allow. The only channel we can use is SMS or GPRS. SMS is not really secure, so the only option we are left with is GPRS. That's not the best way to reach the base of the pyramid as not all phones support that."

The Safaricom position is clear: it spent $30 million to build a business and executed flawlessly, none of the potential dangers (money laundering, terrorist financing, criminal fraud) once envisioned have come to pass, and it should be allowed a chance to recoup its investment and profit before providing access to its crown jewels (merchants and subscribers). "Why would you give your advantage away to your competitor? We put millions into M-PESA," says Michael Joseph. "Why are suddenly all these people saying, 'It must be interoperable?' Because they can't do it by themselves! They want to piggyback on us. That's all. They say it would save money. Come on! We all know why they want it. We made the decision to spend the money, before we earned any money."

Dr. Ndemo, Permanent Secretary of the Ministry of Information and Communication, agrees: "You want to create a revolution, try this. Interoperability would cause delays at the exchange. If you delay Kenyans for one hour you would create a revolution. If it's really just the cost – let the regulator determine how to handle the cost. The moment you begin to share proprietary knowledge, you kill innovation. Even in the healthcare sector, you are given seven years to recoup investments before others can sell generics. This is a worldwide approach to intellectual property. You can't come in two or three years after the fact and say we want to use your system."

REGULATING CASH MERCHANTS AND BANK AGENTS

Another burning policy issue, which pits the banks against M-PESA, is how to devise regulations for cash merchants and bank agents without giving either an unfair advantage. Tangentially related to that is a cry for tiered 'know your customer' (KYC) regulation, which might more easily allow the unbanked to gain access to formal financial services.

In 2010, the Central Bank issued guidelines enabling banks to offer a broad range of banking services through agents (see Chapter 3), in line with Vision 2030's goal of extending financial access to all adult

Kenyans. Bank agents must document 18 months of business ownership, and show adequate capital reserves. According to Njuguna Ndung'u, Governor of the Central Bank, "This innovative mode of banking leverages ICT through the use of mobile phones, point of sale devices, and internet to provide financial services beyond the traditional brick and mortar bank premises."

To date, Equity Bank has been the most aggressive in signing up agents, although not without difficulty. "We are facing problems converting these outlets into what we would be comfortable to call outsourced banks," said James Mwangi, CEO of Equity Bank. "Our agency selection criteria is showing some weaknesses, and we are now reorganising what we demand of agents in order to favour cash heavy operations in order to meet this demand,"

The government response has been to encourage banks to partner with mobile firms, as Equity Bank did with Orange and Yu. "We are encouraging banks to share infrastructure to gain economies of scale and to reduce overheads through increased use of ICT, agency and mobile banking," says Finance Minister, Uhuru Kenyatta.

One interesting outcome may be that a telecom such as Orange forms partnerships with multiple banks, which gives them access to all bank agents, since none can be exclusive to any one bank. That would help Orange quickly build a network to challenge M-PESA, which it clearly cannot do on its own.

In 2011, a year or so after issuing bank agency regulations, the Central Bank issued draft regulations covering "retail payment" agents – aka cash merchants, or M-PESA agents. This precipitated another request from banks to review bank-agent regulations against those of payment agents. Bank agents, for example, had to apply to the Central Bank for a licence, whereas Safaricom has been signing up agents on its own terms and giving the Central Bank a list. The real stickler, for Equity Bank at least, is that banks cannot retain exclusive agents, but have to make them available to other banks. Retail cash merchants, by contrast, have been and can be exclusive to Safaricom and other mobile operators.

Equity Bank and other banks argue that the policy is misguided, because a mobile operator's cash merchants are merely exchanging cash for e-money, while bank agents are selling products specific to their bank. How could a bank agent reliably represent multiple banks? And why couldn't a cash merchant exchange e-money for M-PESA, Orange, Airtel and Yu? After all, the merchant is not representing the telecom, merely providing an add-on service, while a bank agent does fully represent the bank.

"When you talk about bank agents, you are talking about loans, insurance – a higher level of custodial services that requires more training than cash-in/cash-out agents," says Matthew Krueger, a member of the M-Banking Research & Strategy team at Equity Bank "If, say, Barclays is going to have an exclusive agent, whom they train extensively on their product, Equity Bank can have an exclusive agent to train on our product. Today it's the opposite. If we train an agent and invest in the branding, isn't it confusing if, say, Kenya Commercial Bank comes along and offers their product through the same agent? On the other hand, we're happy to share cash-in/cash-out because it's something that doesn't require a huge level of sophistication."

On that count, banks have been partially satisfied, as the Central Bank now allows banks to operate retail cash merchants as well as bank agents. Thus, banks can offer cash-in/cash-out merchants to compete with M-PESA, although they still cannot piggyback on M-PESA's exclusive network. The Central Bank's new retail payments regulation essentially unbundles the different services that cash merchants and bank agents perform – cash-in/cash-out vs. deposit taking – and treats the functions rather than the institutions delivering the function.

Nonetheless, Safaricom has a huge head start over the banks, which are beginning to realize that they need to begin executing on the ground even as they continue to lobby for rule changes. "Banks and formal financial service providers need to get their act together and not let the telcos become significant financial sector players at their expense," says Equity's Staley. "If the banks don't, telcos will be major players in financial services. I don't think this will happen, but it's possible."

Martin Otieno, the CEO of Kenya Commercial Bank, concurs. When asked by Wolfgang Fengler, lead economist in Nairobi for the World Bank, whether he sees M-PESA as a threat or an opportunity, Otieno said, "If you don't respond, it's a threat. But if you embrace it, then it's an opportunity."

Frederik Eijkman, managing director of PEP Intermedius (see Chapter 2), who started as an M-PESA aggregator but now provides agent services for Equity Bank and KCB, feels that banks are making their move. "They are rethinking their business models and products," says Eijkman. "You talk about the poor, the base of the pyramid that Safaricom has exploited so well, this is where banks are looking to focus. I think agents will play a big role because it's too expensive to set up a branch or an ATM. Proximity and accessibility will make the difference."

Michael Klein, former VP Private Sector Development at the World Bank and Chief Economist at the IFC, and now a professor at the Frankfurt School of Finance and Management, agrees with the Governor's "test and learn" approach. He argues that less is more when it comes to regulating cash merchants. "They trade with their own property at risk. They do not put others at risk. Therefore, it would *a priori* seem appropriate to rely on commercial law and the standard resolution mechanism. The service quality is easily observable; the stakes are small; market entry is possible at low cost. Additional governance mechanisms do not seem needed."

The fact of the matter is that anyone with an M-PESA account could offer cash-in/cash-out services, assuming they had enough cash to cover withdrawals. However, the amount of e-money they could sell would be limited by the upper threshold of KShs 70,000 so it wouldn't be much of a business. The point, however, is that no regulation is needed to cover such a basic transaction between two parties trading with their own property (money).

World Bank's Wolfgang Fengler: "The way I see it, renovation follows innovation. We allowed mobile money to happen. You are monitored closely but you are allowed to grow and you aren't stifled by tight regulation. For instance, if every M-PESA agent had to be a bank agent, you wouldn't have seen M-PESA grow, because of the pure fact that banks are not available in many parts of the country."

KNOW YOUR CUSTOMER (KYC) REGULATIONS

The spread of bank agents in small shops and gas stations constitutes branchless banking – or, more accurately, banking beyond branches – and it's clearly crucial to increasing financial access and thus financial inclusion. But before opening a bank account, a bank needs to know certain information about a customer – utility bills, proof of address, photo IDs et al are part of 'know your customer' (KYC) regulations. So what happens if you provide access to a previously unbanked individual who cannot provide identification or proof of income?

For some time now there has been a growing chorus to develop a tiered approach to KYC regulations. For high value accounts, banks and governments want to know who their customers are and where they got their money, as a hedge against money laundering and terrorism financing. Names are matched against a list of suspicious people. But for small accounts below a certain level, money laundering shouldn't be a concern.

In Kenya, where many citizens carry a national identity card, the problem of identification is easily solved. But many citizens working in the informal sector, or from rural villages without street names and addresses, may not be able to provide proof of address. "Even if you can get to a bank branch, you'd need to prove your address with a utility bill," says Seema Desai, director of GSMA's MMU programme. "To be very practical about this, not everybody in developing markets will have a utility bill or even a permanent address."

"We need a risk based KYC regime," says Equity's Staley. "In Haiti, they allow anyone to open an account, and then they measure the cumulative value of transactions and the amount of money sitting in the accounts. As long as the limits are low, who cares? So let's have risk based KYC, where banks can open accounts for everybody. Once you reach a certain limit, we send you an SMS saying, "We see you are using this product but you can't continue using it until you provide XYZ documentation. People say, 'She hasn't got a fixed address because she looks like a nomad'. But what are the chances of her funding Al Qaida? Very low. And if she does start funding Al Qaida, we'll pick it up."

The value of mobile money to society is no longer a technological issue or a demand issue. Mobile money works, and people use it. The upside is high, and it's hard to see a downside. But mobile money is still fragile, and its value and rate of innovation could be stifled by corporate or regulatory mismanagement, let alone a major incident of fraud, money laundering or terrorism financing. On this count, the Central Bank of Kenya's "test and learn" approach has been exemplary and effective.

Chapter 8
KENYA ON STAGE

Nairobi – The Brookings Institution in Washington has been playing host to a top-level conference effectively celebrating Kenya. Governors of central banks, top executives from The World Bank, State Department, U.S. Treasury, White House, Bill & Melinda Gates Foundation and leading universities assembled to examine how to expand financial inclusion using new technologies. Yet, at the very core of it, this parley was about Kenya.

How, as a presenter posed, has a poor country on the right hand side of the map of Africa revolutionized the use of mobile phones as a store of value and most importantly as a vehicle to bring virtually all the unbanked population into a sophisticated payment system.

How can this be copied? The eloquent presentations by The Governor of Kenya's Central Bank, The Head of CCK and Michael Joseph (in his new capacity as Fellow of The World Bank) understandably got rapt attention.

To benchmark our achievement, we must do the unusual and acknowledge heroes who are not waheshimiwa (honourable). The M-PESA revolution marked the meeting of three bold movers who were ready to take very major risks in innovation.

The unsung hero of this innovation was Dr Bitange Ndemo, the Permanent Secretary at Communications Ministry, who in a letter late in 2006, urged his colleague at the Treasury to host a meeting of his team, Treasury and Central Bank to explore something he already saw as a challenge and opportunity bigger than any one agency of government could handle on its own.

Without a successful precedent to emulate, Safaricom's Michael Joseph took the gamble to invest US $30 million in using a phone to send and receive money; something only The Philippines had attempted half heartedly and an investment they assumed would take many years to recoup.

At the Central Bank, Prof Ndung'u had the audacity not only to ignore the deafening scare mongering of the big banks, and scepticism among high government people, but to point out that facilitative regulation sometimes entails allowing innovations to go ahead even when the law for regulating it is not yet in place.

In the mix of this come the Kenyan people. Long used to costly and risky forms of moving money and untapped by the banks, they embraced mobile money much more than even the initiators could have dreamt.

Mukhisa Kituyi, Director of The Kenya Institute of Governance, and Visiting Fellow at The Brookings Institution

****

Mobile money first started in The Philippines in 2003 and later spread to South Africa, but since M-PESA's success, more than 100 other new programmes have launched in over 125 countries; another 100 are on the launch pad. None come close to matching M-PESA's success. Yet.

Why Africa? Why Kenya? Was it flawless execution? Is it possible to recreate M-PESA in another country? If so, why hasn't it been done? "Surely this can and must be replicated in other similar countries, many of which have better starting conditions than we had in Kenya," says Michael Joseph, who since his retirement as CEO has become a global mobile money booster for the World Bank and later Vodafone. True, but so far, false.

Disappointment in the scale and impact of mobile money is real. Part of the problem has been caused by the expectation that mobile money would automatically and effectively "bank the unbanked." But unlike microfinance, which was also overhyped as a way to end poverty, mobile money must scale quickly if it is to actually take hold, let alone deliver results. Thus, in looking forward, the focus should be first on the business implementation to scale and profit, rather than the notion of financial inclusion.

Providers also need to take a broader view of the mobile money ecosystem. Most telecoms typically see mobile money as an opportunity to cross-sell another service to their existing customers, and in the process create stickiness for prepaid mobile services, which carry no contracts. Most banks, meanwhile, see branchless banking as an opportunity to reduce the cost of servicing their existing customers.

The complexity of mobile money services requires that both actors approach the idea more holistically. The idea is not just to maintain or acquire customers but to deliver sufficient value to stores that are acting as cash merchants, and to businesses managing employees and supply chains. Without a broader perspective that includes ecosystem development, most providers will not have the wherewithal to drive mobile money or branchless banking forward at sufficient scale and speed.

SCALING THE NETWORK

Historically, financial innovations have been adopted slowly. Credit cards in the developed world, for example, were first introduced in the 1950s, but it wasn't until the 1980s that credit cards began to reach critical mass. In 30 years, microcredit has extended loans to a mere 200 million people. Mobile money is moving much faster than that, thanks to familiarity with airtime scratch cards and transfer, and has reached 40 million people in seven years (15 million of which are through M-PESA). Many people who have never engaged with the formal financial sector have quickly accepted as fact the concept that they can convert cash into abstract value in a phone, and share that value with others.

The M-PESA model has been carefully scrutinized. In retrospect, analysts can tick off a litany of reasons for its success: Vodafone's determination to reframe the business opportunity based on customer feedback during the pilot; natural urban-rural remittance patterns; the high cost of existing money transfer options; Safaricom's dominant market share and its all-out marketing blitz; the enterprising nature of Kenyans in building an agent network and adopting new applications for M-PESA; a Central Bank that watched carefully but did not stifle innovation; and supportive senior management at Safaricom.

M-PESA was brilliantly deployed, and sped from pilot to rollout to scale. M-PESA was a pure mobile play, not hindered by a complex relationship with a bank, the Achilles heel of many other mobile money implementations. Mobile money, like mobile telephony itself, is dependent on achieving a network effect. For the mobile operator, maintaining a system that does not scale is prohibitively expensive – which is why banks have not served the rural poor for centuries!

Mobile operators depend on millions of small transactions. Without that, mobile money is merely an annoying diversion from the core business of providing voice and text (SMS) capability. Scaling requires investment, primarily to build a technology platform and to acquire customers – Safaricom invested an estimated $30 million over three years to launch M-PESA – but CEOs are often hesitant to invest until the business case has been made. Whatever the reason, inability to scale has been the bugaboo of many of the world's mobile money schemes.

"A large investment in marketing, sends a signal to potential users, of commitment. This service is here to stay, and so you can count on more and more people joining the network in the future," notes the GSMA Development Fund's Mobile Money for the Unbanked, in its 2011 Annual Report. "Second, making a big splash in a shorter time period makes more sense than investing the same amount of money into a longer, lower intensity campaign. This is an axiom in marketing that is even more important when network effects are at play because the goal is to bring lots of customers onto the platform in a short period of time, minimizing the period during which the small number of registered users makes joining seem relatively unattractive to everyone else."

"If you do a pilot with 100 people and it is working, there is no need to expand the pilot to 1,000 people," says consultant Ignacio Mas. "The next step is a fast, national rollout that scales quickly. The only possible exception is a country like India, where you might want to scale state by state before going national."

A FILIPINO INNOVATION

Prepaid cards, starting in the late 1990s, set the stage for mobile money. The first hint of what we know today as mobile money got its start in The Philippines in 2000 (sometimes called the SMS capital of the world), when Smart Communications introduced Smart Money, in partnership with Banco do Oro. Users with a bank account could transfer money from their accounts to a Smart Money account on their phone, making it the world's first reloadable e-wallet. Subscribers could then text Smart Money to other Smart Money subscribers, such as taxi drivers or food outlets.

In 2003, Smart built on Smart Money with Smart Load, which enabled electronic transfer of airtime (as opposed to scratch cards) from resellers to subscribers. Prepaid text and call combo packages were sold in increments as low as 54 cents – what Smart called "telecom in sachets" (small packages). This was in keeping with Smart's relentless focus on marketing to the base of the pyramid. Smart essentially integrated the Smart Money value loading technology into the prepaid reseller system – the opposite of what M-PESA and others have done since, in leveraging the prepaid network to drive mobile money.

Since then, Smart has opened up Smart Money to everyone, bank account or not, after a fairly simple "know your customer" application process. While Banco do Oro still provides the backbone for cash transfers, Smart wireless centres do the same. Many even provide automatic agents, kind of mobile money ATMs, where people put cash into a machine that loads e-money onto their phones. Without doubt, similar machines will eventually replace human agents, at least in cities, around the world. Rural areas will still suffer from the last mile syndrome.

In 2004, Globe Telecom, Smart's only competitor, introduced G-Cash. Globe had targeted the upper end of the market, but clearly needed to respond to Smart's mobile money moves. G-Cash turned your phone into a wallet – and you didn't need a bank account. G-Cash was a pure mobile play. You had to visit a Globe business centre or resellers to exchange cash for e-float, as you now do with M-PESA agents. You could even pay certain retailers, such as 7-Eleven and McDonald's, and pay bills and taxes. Over time, both Filipino carriers expanded to allow international money transfer (remittances from the UK) and repayment of microloans. But Smart, the first mover, has won the subscriber war, with 8.5 million users, to Globe's 1 million.

There are three plausible explanations for why neither carrier has come close to M-PESA's 15 million subscribers, even though The Philippines' population of 101 million dwarfs Kenya's 41 million. One, the commissions for selling airtime in The Philippines are far superior to those for selling mobile money, roughly 12% to 1%. Why would a reseller even think about mobile money? Two, the existing money transfer services in The Philippines were far superior to those in Kenya, so there was less of a market void to fill. Three, the majority of remittances to The Philippines come from overseas, as migrants in search of work find it in the U.K., India and the Middle East.

MOBILE MONEY SPREADS TO SOUTHERN AFRICA

South Africa is by far the richest country in sub-Saharan Africa, but income is not very evenly distributed and less than 50% of South Africans have bank accounts. In many rural areas, you can drive 100 miles without seeing a bank. The mobile phone penetration rate, however, is in the high 90's.

The first mobile-banking application in South Africa was started by MTN Communications (one of the first black owned corporations post apartheid) in 2003, through a joint venture with Standard Bank, similar to the Smart bank-partner model. (In both cases, branding was in the name of the mobile operator.) MTN Banking customers were customers of Standard Bank who could use their phones to interact with the bank and to transfer money. Customers received an ATM card, upgradeable to a MasterCard debit card. Much later, after M-PESA started, MTN rolled out MTN MobileMoney in eight other African countries (Benin, Botswana, Cameroon, Cote d'Ivoire, Ghana, Rwanda, Uganda, Swaziland). Outside of South Africa, you generally do not need a bank account to use MTN MobileMoney.

Celpay, a former subsidiary of Celtel (now Bharti Airtel) and now independent, is neither a bank nor a mobile operator, but works with both to forge mobile money products in the Democratic Republic of Congo, Zambia and Tanzania. Celpay, which started in Zambia in 2001, has been through several iterations, but has of late settled on a business to business model, offering distributors, who typically deal in cash, a way to provide electronic payments to suppliers. Celpay's strongest market remains Zambia.

WIZZIT, like Celpay, is neither a bank nor a telecom, but an integrator that provides a platform that multiple banks and telecoms can use to connect their customers. Launched in 2004, as a division of the

South African Bank of Athens, WIZZIT is independently owned. Customers don't need a bank account, but can deposit cash at post offices that act as agents, and can withdraw funds from any ATM branch, using WIZZIT's Maestro branded debit card. WIZZIT's salesforce is made up of previously unemployed university graduates, from low income communities, known as "WIZZ Kids." This feelgood story, however, has not resulted in much uptake – well under 1 million customers in seven years.

THE THAI MODEL

In 2005, True Move, a mobile operator in Thailand, introduced True Money, which now has 6 million customers who process nearly $1 billion in electronic payments a year. True Group is a converged communications provider that offers mobile, landline, cable TV, internet, WIFI, and online gaming services. In creating its e-wallet, True Group was partially responding to a critical internal problem: how to make it easier for customers to buy its various prepaid services. Thus, True Money started as a payments system rather than a money-transfer system, which is saturated in Thailand with numerous low cost options from banks and post offices. However, as M-PESA's transfer system has been extended into payments, True Money's payment system has extended from payments into transfers.

Like M-PESA, True Money is embedded on the True Move SIM card, making registration quite convenient; it can be done electronically without visiting an agent. Unlike M-PESA, True Money cannot be loaded with cash; only 'cash cards' (airtime scratch cards), credit cards, and direct links from any bank account. (Regulations in Thailand do not allow customers to withdraw money from an e-wallet on a mobile phone.) Even though the majority of Thais are banked, the cash card is the number one option. Because of this, airtime resellers are big promoters of True Money, and also sell the multipurpose True Money Cash Cards, even though they earn a lower commission than from airtime cards. True convinced dealers that the high volume generated by its payments system would more than make up for the lower commission. And since True Money is primarily a payments system, it does not face the issue of cashing out, as M-PESA does.

Thus, the landscape pre-M-PESA has three major players: Smart Money in The Philippines, MTN Banking in South Africa and True Money in Thailand. All were gradations on the theme of a connection between a mobile operator and a bank, greased by the airtime reseller as an intermediary. None were "pure mobile plays" like M-PESA. The landscape post-M-PESA is not unlike the pre-M-PESA landscape, in terms of hybrid mobile money applications, except that it is extremely crowded. That includes several M-PESA clones sparked by Vodafone.

M-PESA CLONES

After the launch of M-PESA and its meteoric uptake, Nick Hughes's role at Vodafone changed from Director of Social Enterprise to Head of International Mobile Payments. His group focused on other countries where some variant of M-PESA might take hold. The Holy Grail, as for many consumer marketers, was India. Half the team focused on cracking the code that would enable mobile money service in a country of more than 1 billion people, where today more people have mobile phones than have toothbrushes. The code has not yet been cracked, although M-PESA is on the ground.

Another country of interest to Vodafone was Egypt, which looked quite promising. Fewer than 20% of Egyptians have bank accounts, domestic remittances are not unlike those in Kenya, the government and Central Bank are making noise about going cashless, fewer than one in 10 have credit cards and mobile penetration is increasing rapidly (nearly 80%). But the project was slow to develop, in large part due to government intransigence. In May 2011, not long after the Tahrir Square uprising, the Central Bank approved mobile operators to launch money-transfer services, although security concerns are still an issue and Vodafone indicated it planned to launch a service.

The first M-PESA service Vodafone actually launched outside Kenya was in 2008 in Tanzania, Kenya's neighbour to the south. Vodafone is a 65% stakeholder in Vodacom of South Africa, which in turn is a 65% stakeholder in Vodacom Tanzania. Geographically, Tanzania is about twice the size of Kenya, with roughly the same population (42 million to Kenya's 41 million), but Tanzania is even more rural, and the middle of the country is thinly populated. Because of that dispersion and also for cultural reasons (Tanzanians are more nationalistic, Kenyans more family and tribally oriented), the natural urban-rural remittance patterns that drove M-PESA in Kenya are less prevalent in Tanzania.

Vodacom Tanzania's market share of roughly 40% is far below Safaricom's 80% in Kenya, and it has half as many subscribers (10 million versus 20 million). Since Vodacom launched, three competitors have joined the fray – Bharti Airtel, Tigo (Millicom) and Zantel (Etisalat). Combined, these factors make it more difficult to develop a strong network effect. Nonetheless, Vodacom has garnered 7 million subscribers in three years, although these are automatic signups with a SIM purchase, and the numbers of active users is said to be less than 2 million. "I wish it was as easy as putting up a billboard in every dusty village in Tanzania," says Jacques Voogt, Head of Vodafone M-PESA in Tanzania. "But it's a lot harder – it's about guys walking around the villages with a T-shirt saying, 'Ask me about M-PESA!' and striking up conversations. It's about canopies in front of agent shops and a massive focus on educating one potential customer at a time."

About the same time Vodafone was deploying M-PESA in Tanzania, it was rolling out M-PAISA in Afghanistan, through mobile operator Roshan, which is majority owned by the Aga Khan Foundation for Economic Development. Needless to say, Afghanistan is a tough market aside from the ongoing war, with rugged mountains, dispersed villages, widespread thievery, and a 70% illiteracy rate. Initially, M-PAISA was targeted at microfinance groups and later, as a way of person to person transfers and also to distribute police salaries. When policemen first started receiving electronic paychecks, they were surprised their salary payments were a third larger than they had previously received. The perceived increase in pay was what a paycheck looked like without corrupt bosses skimming cash off the top! One police chief went so far as to steal the SIM cards of his officers so he could skim money off their mobile phones.

Zahir Khoja, CEO of Roshan, is one of the more passionate and charismatic CEOs in the mobile money arena, and with the Aga Khan Foundation has made Roshan a powerful social force, focusing on education, health and jobs. And Roshan's Interactive Voice Response system (in Dari, Pashto and English), implemented to deal with the high illiteracy rate, is an innovative approach to contextual marketing. But it's not clear that M-PAISA will gain a real toehold any time soon. To date, M-PAISA has attracted just over 100,000 subscribers, and is stuck in the subscale trap that drains operators' resources without delivering revenues.

Vodacom South Africa, 65% owned by Vodafone and one of the bigger mobile operators on the continent, didn't introduce M-PESA until the second half of 2010. Susie Lonie, who had helped launch M-PESA in Kenya and Tanzania, was the lead manager in Vodacom South Africa. She was initially expected to sign up 10 million M-PESA users within three years, an ambitious target given that the total unbanked population in South Africa is 13 million, and MTN MobileMoney is already well established. Vodacom's bank partner is Nedbank, but the product is aimed at the unbanked. M-PESA started very slowly, signing up less than 150,000 subscribers in the first six months, and Vodafone has since decided to try a new marketing tack, aiming more upmarket.

Assessing Vodafone's M-PESA clones, Vodacom Tanzania has achieved by far the best traction, although South Africa would appear to offer the best potential for explosive growth. In India, Vodafone Essar (67% owned by Vodafone) has more than 130 million mobile customers, but M-PESA is still in pilot phase. Even for Vodafone, co-architect of the world's biggest mobile money success, spinning off scalable and profitable new ventures is not a cookie-cutter affair.

101 ITERATIONS AND COUNTING

The big African telecom players, in addition to Vodafone/Vodacom, are South Africa's MTN, India's

Bharti Airtel, and France's Orange. Bharti's Airtel Money, which it inherited when it bought Zain in 2010, is a clear descendant of M-PESA, starting in Kenya, Tanzania, and Uganda in 2009, then moving a year later into Ghana, Madagascar, Malawi, Niger, Sierra Leone, and Zambia.

Similarly, France Telecom Group's Orange, which operates in Kenya, opened Orange Cash in Cote d'Ivoire in 2009, then a year later moved its Orange Cash in 2010 into Kenya, Madagascar, Mali, Niger, and Senegal. It seems only a matter of time before mobile money spreads to all 52 countries in Africa, just as mobile phones did a decade ago.

Outside Africa, the countries experimenting with mobile money read like a random list culled from United Nations membership: Haiti, Guatemala, Cambodia, Indonesia, Fiji, Georgia, Jordan, Vietnam, Tonga, Mongolia, Sri Lanka, Bangladesh....

In the so-called BRICs – Brazil, Russia, India, and China – which account for close to half the world's population, mobile money has yet to take hold. Nokia Easy Pay and Easy Send, in conjunction with YES Bank, is up and running in India, but without scale, and M-PESA is still developing. ("For Vodafone, India will be the biggest market," says Michael Joseph, who is now director of mobile payments at Vodafone. "It is really right for this product.") China Mobile, the world's largest telecom in revenues (with 500 million subscribers), bought a 20% stake in Shanghai Pudong Development Bank, with the presumed intention of introducing mobile money transfers and payments. In Russia, there is no activity; in Brazil, financial inclusion has taken a different form, what strategists would call an "adjacency" market: branchless banking.

Banks rather than mobile operators have driven banking beyond branches in Brazil, and Latin America generally. Brazil has nearly 200,000 retail outlets with point-of-sale terminals that process bills, and offer credit and insurance, as well as cash withdrawals. Caixa Economica Federal, one of the big mass market banks, counts six times as many cash merchants as branches. There are roughly twice as many bank "correspondents" (as the Brazilians refer to agents) in Brazil as in Kenya; 82 per 100,000 people compared to 45 per 100,000, according to David Porteous, CEO of Bankable Frontiers, a global consultancy. But Brazil also has more bank branches per 100,000 than Kenya (13 to 4), and has been building its correspondent network for more than a decade.

Elsewhere in Latin America, Peru ranks second to Brazil in number of agents, with close to 6,000, led by Banco de Credito del Peru. Regulators in Colombia allowed cash merchants at the beginning of 2007 and BanColombia, the largest bank, has built a network of more than 600 cash merchants. In Mexico, where regulations changed in 2009, Banco Wal-Mart was the first bank authorized to operate through retail agents at its 1,400 Wal-Mart stores.

TRACTION IN TANZANIA, UGANDA AND PAKISTAN

The ultimate winners and losers will be determined by three key factors: the will of major mobile operators to use their muscle (money and network) to quickly scale; the willingness of Central Banks, financial regulators and lawmakers to lay out clear guidelines that both facilitate innovation and protect customers; the degree of collaboration between mobile operators and banks in reaching out to new markets.

It's still early in the game, but several mobile money services are gaining traction. Vodacom Tanzania's M-PESA, mentioned earlier, is one. Beyond that, two services merit special attention: Telenor's Easypaisa ("easy money") in Pakistan, and MTN's MobileMoney in Uganda.

MTN was an early mobile money actor with its 2004 South African MTN Banking, and now has mobile money operations in nine African countries. MTN Uganda's MobileMoney launched in partnership with Stanbic Bank in 2009; less than two years later, it had 1.5 million subscribers and 2,500 agents.

Uganda has a slightly smaller population than Kenya (35 million to 41 million), but is much poorer, with a GDP half of Kenya's. MTN is the market leader in Uganda, with a better than 40% share, but the market is fragmented – Bharti Airtel, Warid and Uganda Telecom hover a little below 20%, and Orange has a tiny slice of the market. When it launched, MTN MobileMoney allowed transfers to recipients on any network, and that has helped them grow quickly and drive revenues, for transfers out-of-network incur a 7% to 94% premium, depending on the size of transfer.

In its first year and a half, MTN MobileMoney signed up 17% of MTN's voice customers (M-PESA's rate was 31%), and was cash flow positive, according to a case study analysis by the GSMA Development Fund's Mobile Money for the Unbanked. The majority of revenues (52%) are driven by transactions, but indirect contributions are almost as important. Savings from airtime distribution, reduction in churn and increased share of wallet for voice and SMS. Moreover, after the first year, fixed costs (building the platform, marketing, embedding the application on SIM cards) as a percentage of spending were reduced to 34%.

Taken together, this data suggests that MTN MobileMoney achieved scale fast enough to justify continued investment. And, while it did invest $10 million in the first 14 months, it is already seeing returns that will pay that down quickly. MobileMoney has added bill payments for pay TV and water, and expects to reach 3.5 million subscribers in 2012.

The landscape is quite different in Pakistan. It's a huge country (188 million) and, while poor, its per capita GDP is twice that of Uganda. Pakistan has twice as many bank branches per 100,000 as Kenya (9 to 4). But in 2008, the State Bank of Pakistan issued regulations ("Branchless Banking Regulations for Financial Institutions Desirous to Undertake Branchless Banking") that explicitly forbade mobile operators from offering mobile financial services. It also specified parts of the value chain – for example, risk management – that a bank could not outsource, and others, such as agent network management, which it could.

When Norway based Telenor, which operates in 14 countries, entered Pakistan in 2005, it already had eight years worth of experience in Bangladesh (formerly East Pakistan) building out GrameenPhone, in which it holds a majority stake. Telenor, now the largest European investor in Pakistan, has built a subscriber base of 25 million, making it the number two carrier in Pakistan behind Orascom.

In 2006, Telenor had introduced mobile bill payments in Bangladesh, a service it planned to port to Pakistan. However, the State Bank's ruling effectively killed that plan – unless Telenor were to buy a bank.

And so it did – a 51% share in Tameer Microfinance Bank. Tameer received capital to invest in Easypaisa, but also for its core banking business. Telenor gained an entrée to mobile banking – and a half share in any collective profits.

Despite restrictive "know your customer" requirements, making account opening difficult, Telenor and Tameer quickly built a very successful mobile money operation. In its first year, Easypaisa signed up several million subscribers and 8,000 agents, and processed 5 million transactions, bill payments and money transfers. Easypaisa has also launched a remittance service with Xpress Money in the United Kingdom, for families to send money home to Pakistan. Two competitors, Mobilink (Orascom) and UBL Bank, lag behind Easypaisa's fast start.

Back in Bangladesh, a promising startup called bKash launched in 2011, aimed at both banked and unbanked customers. A hybrid partnership between mobile operator Robi Axiata and BRAC Bank, bKash was started by CEO Kamal Quadir. Quadir previously built and sold Cell Bazaar, a kind of mobile Craig's List for GrameenPhone subscribers. bKash, backed by a $10 million grant from the Bill & Melinda Gates Foundation, is built on the Fundamo platform for mobile money that is used in 40 countries.

****

"What are the lessons of Kenya's ICT revolution for the broader economy of Kenya and for other countries? First, this revolution is not just for the young tech-savvy programmers that huddle at iHub. ICT is no longer a niche sector of the economy. It has become mainstream and affects virtually every actor and every sector of the economy. It's misleading to talk

about a so-called "new economy" because it has in fact changed the way the old economy is operating. Over the next years, the biggest innovations will probably come from the incubation of technology in "traditional" sectors. The financial sector is already in the midst of this transformation, with mobile money as the most visible sign.

Second, the mobile revolution can become a game changer for the poor. Mobile money presents an unparalleled opportunity to deliver a basic suite of modern financial services to unbanked billions across the world. It is amazing to observe how the mobile phone has morphed from a luxury tool into a household item and become one of the most powerful weapons in the fight against poverty.

Kenyans should take pride in this development because they remain at the forefront of ICT innovation globally. There are some 35 million mobile money users in the world today: one in two is a Kenyan. Mobile money took off in Kenya thanks to a combination of strong leadership and vision in business and government. And this won't be the last time that an African country is a world market leader and an exporter of innovation!"

Wolfgang Fengler, Lead Economist, World Bank (Nairobi)

Chapter 9
CASH IS THE ENEMY!

"A 'high road' scenario sees Kenya dramatically reducing its dependence on cash – a key source of cost – shifting to a "cash-lite" economy with electronic payments replacing all but the smallest value transactions. For this to occur, the Kenyan economy will need to get over the 'hump' – the point at which cash is no longer used as intensively since people are able to transact electronically, so that the demand for cash in and cash out transactions declines. But for this to happen, there are several prerequisites. Formal financial services must reach well beyond urban markets where they are concentrated today. The delivery channels to support this outreach must be both ubiquitous and low cost/affordable. To reach the position where most people have and can use an electronic account requires that first, the 'wheels of cash' must be 'greased': it must be made as easy and as cheap as possible to convert cash to electronic value, and vice versa. This means that there must be a wide range of locations at which customers can deposit and withdraw cash: bank branches, ATMs and retailers (banking agents and other types of cash handling outlets). Until the "cash-lite" scenario is realized, financial providers need every incentive to acquire cash-handling agents, agents need incentives to handle cash and customers must have good reasons to use their local agents."

Stephen Mwuara Nduati, Head of National Payments Systems, Central Bank of Kenya

****

People like cash. They can touch it, feel it and see it. Cash equals stature. The bigger the wad, the better. There's nothing like the immediate transfer of paper and coin from hand to hand. No deferred gratification, no signature needed, no question of trust. Cash used to be teeth and shells, then metal and paper. In whatever form, it is tactile and elemental, almost a part of our earth and certainly a glue to our social structure.

In the West, where plastic has taken reign, cash is dying off. In Africa, it's impossible to get by without it. Even the rich rarely use plastic; and most merchants don't accept it. Cash is still king in Africa, where people abhor debt and credit, even when they can get it. But in an electronic age, cash is truly the enemy – for governments, businesses, and poor people. The transaction costs of cash are just too high.

Cash is the enemy of governments, which must print and reprint, then transport it. In Singapore, an Asian Banker survey found cash cost the government more than $1 billion in 2006. In Kenya, the cost of insuring cash has risen materially in recent years, after a spate of high profile armed robberies.

Cash is the enemy of banks, which must build bricks and mortar vaults staffed by dozens of clerks and guards to handle, process and store it. Cash is the enemy of businesses, which waste time and money moving cash to suppliers and paying workers. And they lose huge amounts of cash to theft and corruption.

Cash is even the enemy of mobile money providers, because it forces operators to share almost half their revenues with retail stores whose only job is to provide backward compatibility with the legacy payment system – cash. "Take cash out, and mobile money could be so much cheaper and so much more profitable," says consultant Mas.

Finally, cash is most particularly the enemy of the poor, who struggle to get it, hide it, keep it. Cash is hard to transmit, especially to remote areas; cash is dangerous to carry or even to stash in not so secret locations; cash is tempting to spend, even for very disciplined people. And dealing exclusively in cash makes it impossible to build a credit rating.

For the hundreds of millions of small farmers , who operate far off the electronic grid in a physical world of animals and vegetables but lack even rudimentary irrigation systems, for the hundreds of millions of casual labourers, who limp from day to day and job to job ("the poor are rich in jobs"), for the hundreds of millions of micro entrepreneurs who are desperate for capital, and for the hundreds of millions of pastoralists, who pray for rain and suffer when it doesn't, cash is what they know and need. But cash is their enemy because of the high transaction costs to procure and store and borrow it.

Imagine the opportunities that would open up for poor people everywhere if their cash were "dematerialized" and treated purely as information. Digital money – mere digits on a server – is easier to conceal, transport, and deliver than physical cash. Digital money leaves information in its wake, which can be used automatically to build up financial histories for individuals or accounting records for businesses.

Were the branchless banking infrastructure to become sufficiently pervasive, it could be thought of as a utility that links citizens and enterprises to each other and to a range of formal financial and non-financial service providers. The payment infrastructure would equate to an information utility that would ride on top of mobile networks.

Dematerializing cash would give entrepreneurs a viable platform on which to develop rich products to serve different segments of the population, and might begin to make financial inclusion a reality. That version of financial inclusion is not likely to look like the one we now envision – some sort of expansive banking system that pushes standard bank products. It is likely to assume a whole new set of characteristics based on usage needs and local customs, which is precisely what happened with the spread of mobile phones.

"If we want financial inclusion, we have to go cashless," says Equity Bank's Staley. "To really bank the unbanked we need to go cashless because the biggest cost of doing financial transactions is actually cash."

In Kenya, mobile money has begun to break the dependence on cash, just as plastic has done in the West. Mobile money has made transfers faster, more secure and less costly. It has given people the opportunity to build credit history. Pay Bill is revolutionizing payments for numerous Kenyan institutions. A reverse payments system, Bulk Payments, has the same impact. Organisations with branches across the country, with thousands of employees, no longer have to worry about delivering cash payments. For factories, flower farms and other industries that have typically paid cash to their workers and suppliers, many of whom do not have bank accounts, Bulk Payments automates the process. And Buy Goods, which several of Kenya's top retail chains use, allows cash free purchasing.

In the recent past, organisations offering subscription based services, such as Kenya Power and Lighting Company (KPLC), set up banking halls for customers to come and pay. Others partnered with supermarkets and petrol stations. These options involved huge operational costs, including security guards. For organisations with remote operations that needed to disburse payments, the best option was to hire a vehicle and send a driver with the money. It's as if every company was running two businesses – the core business providing a product or service, and a collection and/or payments business that dealt monthly with tens of thousands of minute sums of cash. Now, more than 15% of all KPLC payments are via M-PESA, saving both the utility and its customers significant time and money.

Most importantly, mobile money has helped people in a cash culture – and often very poor people – break the psychological bond with cash and accept an SMS as a tradable value. That is a huge leap forward in trust, which is the essence of money. As historian Niall Ferguson notes in The Ascent of Money, money is not metal or paper. "It is trust inscribed. And it does not seem to matter much where it is inscribed: on silver, on clay, on paper, on a liquid crystal display," writes Ferguson. "Anything can serve as money, from the cowrie shells of the Maldives to the huge stone discs used on the Pacific islands of Yap. And now, it seems in this electronic age nothing can serve as money too."

The Kenyan experience has been largely positive, even if it is a first step toward eradicating cash. But – and it's a big "but" – Kenyans are by and large using mobile money as if it were cash! The actual e-money loop – the amount of time money remains in the phone – is actually quite short. For the most part, the cycle is deposit, transfer, withdraw. While money transfer is sped up at reduced cost, which is a huge benefit, the deposit and withdrawal of cash is a costly transaction.

THE E-MONEY LOOP

"I don't see us replacing the banks," says Michael Joseph. "I don't see us going into the mortgage business, into the big loan business, buying a motorcar, buying a house. We will always stay within our frame where each transaction is not more than $300 or $400. Our aim is to bring about a situation where M-PESA subscribers will leave home with money in their M-PESA accounts and not need any other form of cash to transact during the day. The only time you really need big money is when want to go and buy a house. So then you go to a bank. But for your basic daily needs, you don't need this bank."

That's the future dream, not the present reality. Imagine a cash loop as being the amount of time cash circulates after being withdrawn from a bank and before being re-deposited. The e-money loop is the electronic equivalent – the number of transactions that the average unit of mobile money goes through between being deposited as cash and withdrawn as cash. After some mathematical gymnastics, academics Isaac Mbiti (Southern Methodist University) and David Weil (Brown University) conclude that the current e-money loop in Kenya is close to 1 – money is deposited, sent, and withdrawn, with few exceptions. This is really no different than a cash transfer, except for the mode of transfer.

Extensive financial diaries of M-PESA and non-M-PESA users essentially confirm this statistical finding. An indepth study of 92 low income (median income of roughly $2 a day) individuals in three locations across Kenya recorded 18,000 financial transactions over an 18 month period. "Our data show that almost 70% of money going into an M-PESA account leaves that account before any new money is put in, and that in 88% of those cases, the e-money is converted into cash the same day it is received," say authors Monique Cohen, president of Microfinance Opportunities in Washington, D.C. , and Guy Stuart, a Fellow at the Ash Center, Harvard University. "Only 5.6% of the total value of all reported transactions involved e-money expenditures; the remaining 94.4% were cash transactions."

While the results might be slightly different when considering a higher income demographic, it's a stark reminder that cash is still king, with all its attendant costs. "The more the e-money loop can be lengthened, the more that costs can be reduced for both the service provider and for consumers," the authors write.

For all the talk of M-PESA as a disruptive technology, what would explain this short e-money loop? Why does e-money mimic the cash economy among low income Kenyans? Because, Stuart says, patterns are embedded in pre-existing social and spatial relations. Mobile money transfer is guided by two main parameters – distance and purpose. A graph with "distance" on one axis and "purpose" on the other generates four possible main types of transactions: local household, local business, long distance household, and long distance business. To date, most people will send money at a great distance to someone they already know and trust, such as a long distance household, with whom they can verify that the money was received. These are family to family or family to friend remittances, which are quickly cashed out. And people will send money locally to someone they don't know but are dealing with face to face (local business), as in a buyer-seller transaction. The classic example is paying taxi fares, as drivers prefer e-money to cash for security reasons. But local household and long distance business transactions are few and far between. Until people extend their networks beyond what they are comfortable with today – mobile money won't realise its potential transformative effects.

In this, the use of mobile money is not really any different from any new financial technology. Consider ATMs, credit cards, or internet purchases. Initially, usage is driven by well educated and technologically savvy people who are willing to take risks with their money. Over time, as more and more people are persuaded that the safeguards are protecting them, the usage circles expand.

These financial diaries were recorded in the second and third year of M-PESA by a low income, low education demographic. Over time and with repeated interactions, trust circles can be expected to widen beyond family and local businesses to more distant business buyers and sellers. The e-money loop seems to be longer for a business transaction compared to a household one, and business transactions are larger, and thus result in lower transaction fees (as a percentage of the total sent). And, while the "send money home" remittance market is constrained by the size of family networks and available income, business networks have fewer restraints on growth.

Longer e-money loops save customers money, and they are also very good for mobile money providers. That's because cash in/cash out transactions are costly for the provider; in fact, they are the lowest margin part of the mobile money business, while electronic transactions are the highest. Mobile money analysts Kabil Kumar and Toru Mino estimate that M-PESA earns Safaricom an estimated 18% average gross margin on agent based transactions compared with almost 100% gross margin on electronic only transactions. And in their estimate, M-PESA Kenya's "electronic only" transactions grew 35% faster than agent transactions in 2010. That means the e-money loop is lengthening.

"Growth in electronic transactions per deposit or cash-in presents a tantalizing outcome – but how do we drive more transactions per deposit?" ask Kabir and Mino, on the Consultative Group to Assist the Poor's Technology blog. "Of course, the obvious answer is to have more electronic uses for the deposit. In fact, we think that even for M-PESA Kenya, the reason why we saw increasing transactions per deposit was not because people were sending domestic remittances to a wider range of recipients, but because they were doing other types of transactions. We believe that a large share of these other transactions were in fact small business merchant payments." That means the reason the e-money loop is lengthening is because of more transactions between strangers – moving into new quadrants in the Stuart/Cohen distance/purpose framework.

SQUEEZING OUT CASH

If cash, for all its allure, is clearly the enemy, and if the world's most dynamic mobile money system is not yet weaning people from cash in a significant way, what might move the needle?

There are three key catalysts. One is government, which handles more money than any other institution and acts in its own self interest to rid systems of cash. Government regulators are part of this equation. Another is private sector players – mobile operators, banks and third party software developers – which are doggedly squeezing cash out of transactions, as a first generation payments system moves toward a second generation with more sophisticated products. The third is the pace of technological change, which will make high powered smart phones affordable in developing countries. Already, China is producing smart phones with Near Field Communication (NFC) capability for $10. These relentless forces will quickly change consumer behaviour, as we have already seen with the rapid and widespread adoption of M-PESA.

Add to the above an exogenous force of nature – the increasing youthfulness of the world's population. Demographics, coupled with the spread of data-enabled Internet phones – better technology in the hands of younger people – will really drive mobile money. And it will increase competition by opening up a new channel that is not totally controlled by mobile operators. "The growth of the mobile internet may cause a boom in a new generation of branchless banking providers," notes CGAP's Scenarios for Branchless banking in 2020.

The only countervailing force that might slow this steady march toward a "cash-lite" society is a major meltdown of a mobile money system in which millions somehow lost or felt they lost money, or widespread consumer fraud that undermined confidence (trust) in the system. For branchless banking advocates, this is the "nightmare scenario."

A 2009 Kenyan news report (*Business Nation*) hints at the potential for panic: "A technical hitch in the M-PESA money transfer service caused anxious customers to crowd at service outlets to have their accounts updated. Customers had initially been barred from accessing the premises on safety fears after their demands for an up-to-date reflection of their accounts got boisterous. Several administration police officers were deployed to the centre to boost the effort of private guards in calming the angry crowd."

GOVERNMENT-TO-PERSON (G2P) PAYMENTS

Author Ferguson mentioned the cowrie shell currency of The Maldives, but as it happens, that small island nation of roughly 300,000 people is way beyond cowrie shells. In fact, it is moving towards a fully electronic system of payments and banking. The Maldives wants to eradicate cash because it's expensive to move it from island to island.

Of course, the out of sight, out of mind Maldives could use shark teeth for cash and the rest of the world wouldn't care, but much larger countries are also well on their way to eradicating cash. More than 60 countries have cash transfer programmes that make up a public safety net, reaching hundreds of millions of people around the world. The primary approach is to convert social payments from cash to electronic. This is likely to have a huge impact on eradicating cash, or moving toward a "cash-lite" society, and it will connect many of the unbanked to financial institutions that intermediate payments.

Governments are typically the largest micropayers in a country, and many of these payments go to people living in remote areas, such as teachers in rural schools or pensioners who return to their home village upon retirement. The volume of social welfare payments has also increased substantially in recent years; for instance, those made to demobilized soldiers in the Congo, conditional cash transfers to poor families under the Bolsa Familia Program in Brazil, or subsistence wages paid under the National Rural Employment Guarantee Scheme in India. Branchless banking can therefore enhance the reach and efficiency of government social safety nets and reduce the corruption associated with the administration of these programmes. In many cases, these government to person payments are delivered through banking institutions, which provides another linkage point for the previously unbanked.

In Brazil, switching to electronic benefit cards issued by a state-owned financial institution helped cut the administrative cost of delivering millions of grants nearly sevenfold, from 14.7% to 2.6% of grant value disbursed. The South African Social Security Administration (SASSA) saw its costs of delivering social transfers drop 62% (to less than US$2 per payment) after moving to bank accounts offered by the private banking sector. Mexico, which aims to deliver 100% of all government payments electronically by December 2012, is eyeing a 5% savings. A decree by President Vincente Fox in 2007, setting 2012 as a deadline, instilled a sense of urgency to the project.

In Pakistan, the climate for e-money is developing quickly. In the last few years, as it has suffered horrific earthquake and flood disasters, Pakistan has moved closer and closer to electronic payments for poverty and humanitarian needs. After the floods, VISA and UBL Bank provided 2 million magnetic stripe cards that stored cash value of Rs 100,000 ($1,170); the government determined who was eligible, and established a biometric identification process to receive the card. Recipients can spend their money at stores or withdraw their cash at ATMs or agents that were specially set up to deal with the post-flood situation. Similarly, Pakistan's Benazir Bhutto Income Support programme, which distributes $12 a month to 3 million poor women, has moved from a system of distributing money orders through post offices to cash cards women can use to withdraw funds.

Sarah Rotman, a microfinance analyst at CGAP, notes that existing branchless banking systems grease the wheels for such G2P programmes, although it sometimes works in reverse. In Colombia, the spread of banking correspondents was directly linked to Banco Agrario making payments to Familias en Accion beneficiaries. Similarly, UBL in Pakistan built out its payment capacity to reach flood victims and has since built on that infrastructure to serve customers of its "Omni" branchless banking service.

2G MOBILE MONEY: BEYOND PAYMENTS

G2P payments significantly expand the scale and scope of mobile money, but they are still basic payments – such as remittances, airtime top-up, bill payments and loan repayments rather than sophisticated financial products. The real impact of mobile money will derive from next generation products – micro-savings, micro-credit and micro-insurance – which deliver finance to those who have never used banks.

An Oliver Wyman and PlaNet Finance report (Beyond Payments – Next Generation Mobile banking for the Masses) notes, for example, that introducing commitment driven bundled savings has been effective in boosting activity rates by a factor or two or three. "If the bundled product eliminates a pain point for the consumer, it can catalyze the movement of deposits from under the mattress to a bank." In other words, moving beyond payments to more sophisticated products could, in theory, reduce the conversion back to cash and keep value in electronic form for longer.

SAFARICOM IS BIG GAME

The Economist Intelligence Unit expects sub-Saharan banks to surge in growth during the coming decade. Why? High rates of economic growth, financial deepening to fulfil huge unmet needs for basic financial services and new technologies to provide them – particularly over mobile phones. With 600 million phones, more than America or Europe, and one-tenth of its land mass covered by mobile internet, more than India, mobile money should prosper.

But local banks and telecoms will have to look over their shoulders at new players looking to globalize mobile money. As smart phones become cheaper and data plans more affordable, the Internet opens up as a potential new channel, more secure than SMS or USSD (although not as secure as SIM). Handset manufacturers such as Nokia, which has launched Nokia Money in partnership with Obopay, are looking to develop operator-agnostic services that bypass mobile operators. And Google Wallet runs on Android, another operator-agnostic channel. MasterCard and VISA and Western Union – longtime global e-money players – are eyeing new channels and markets. VISA bought Fundamo, a South African based provider of platform services for mobile money services in 40 countries, and has allied with MTN Mobile Money. It's too early to know how well these and other brands will be able to translate their grandiose visions into practical, trustworthy mobile money schemes that are tailored for local conditions and satisfy local regulators. Certainly they will squeeze more and more cash out of the system.

That said, mobile money has been a real shot in the arm for Kenya. Nairobi's natural role as the business capital of East Africa has been solidified, and it is transforming into a global business capital. Kenyatta International Airport is besieged with hordes of visiting consultants and businesspeople, from Africa and the rest of the world. Everyone wants to witness firsthand the mobile money revolution, to unlock the code and bring it home or to another country.

A country that had merely 500,000 landline phones and 17,000 mobile phones in 1999 now has over 25 million mobile phone users (more than the number of adults), with competition from four major carriers driving prices down. A banking industry that was heavily clustered in urban areas has more than doubled the number of branches and ATMs, with the majority of the growth coming in rural areas. Competition has eroded the share of the largest banks, and driven account costs down. The number of people with access to both formal and "formal other" financial services has increased markedly between 2006 and 2009 – from 26% to 41%. The banking and communications industries are indeed complementary, and both are growing in tandem, while sparking numerous hybrid innovations and entrepreneurial business models.

The value of Safaricom to Kenya cannot be overestimated. Safaricom has created, directly or indirectly, over 40,000 jobs in Kenya, and helped push both cash and increasingly e-money into villages, which sparks more commerce and jobs. And M-PESA has dramatically increased bank liquidity, by pushing money that had long been stored in the metaphorical "mattresses" into trust accounts to back the e-float. The Central Bank, in fact attributes much of the huge oversubscription to the Safaricom IPO, to the excess liquidity waiting for a productive investment opportunity.

However you cut it, Safaricom has been great for Kenya and put the country on the world stage. Says Betty Mwangi, General Manager, Safaricom: "M-PESA is like oxygen to Kenyans." Imagine 50 other countries with huge proportions of unbanked citizens inhaling a similar breath of fresh air into their economies.

****

Like many residents of Kibera, Mercy, a stocky woman with close-cropped hair and bright eyes, comes from a rural "upcountry" area of Kenya. She moved to Kibera 15 years ago, she says, because of low rent and a relative who could help her find a job and a place to live. Her house is a typical Kibera shack with a corrugated tin roof and mud floor. Bed sheets hang from the ceiling to divide the structure into separate sections to afford a measure of privacy to Mercy and the nine other people who, remarkably, all share the 15' x 15' structure. Other occupants include Mercy's husband, five children of her own, and three children belonging to her siblings.

Mercy's husband earns money sporadically as a builder. Her own income tends to be a bit steadier as a fish vendor. She went into that business about 10 years ago because the fish she sells are native to her home area near Lake Victoria, and she knew she could capitalize on personal connections with suppliers. She also appreciates the fact that fish supply does not vary with the season – unlike fresh produce, for example. Before the fish business, she sold groceries along a main road on the outskirts of Kibera, which she describes as a much less consistent income.

Mercy has built what she describes as a very stable client base for her wholesale fish business through personal relationships with customers who come to her house to socialize and buy the fish. Her income from fish sales has increased steadily over the last several years (with the exception of the postelection riots in 2007/early 2008 which she says cost her an estimated $400 in lost revenue). She bought her first cell phone in 2002; it immediately became her primary means of communicating with fish suppliers and arranging sales. Deals could be set up through the phone, but payments had to be made in person – either by travelling upcountry herself or entrusting the money to someone else.

About three years ago, Mercy added M-PESA to her portfolio. Her reasons for signing up initially were to send money to relatives and to store money for short periods. Nowadays, the majority of Mercy's use of M-PESA is business related. She generally makes all of her stock purchases through the phone – calling the suppliers upcountry, and then sending the payment via M-PESA. From October 2010 to March 2011 (the second phase of the Financial Diaries study period), she recorded 16 business related remittances to suppliers around Lake Victoria, totalling about $300. She says that the ability to make affordable, reliable remote payments has boosted her bottom line significantly.

Her fish sales often occur in cash. If individual sales are small, she will allow them to accumulate into larger lump sums and then deposit the money into her M-PESA account. She made a total of 17 such business related deposits into M-PESA, with a total value of $570 (average size $34). Mercy also received 31 payments from customers over the study period. The total value was $1,217 and the average was $39. This suggests, interestingly, that many more customers, even local ones, are choosing to pay by M-PESA rather than cash. M-PESA, in effect, serves as Mercy's accounting tool. It provides figures for how much fish she should buy based on the sales revenue deposited on the phone. She also uses M-PESA to make payments on a small enterprise loan to Kenya Women's Finance Trust. In addition, Mercy employs M-PESA in a variety of functions not related to her fish business. For example, she receives household funds that her husband earns working construction jobs away from their home. Most of her other transactions are outgoing cash transfers. She sends the tuition for her children directly to the schools via M-PESA. She also sends money home to her parents about once per month; they use the funds to support general household expenses. More recently, she had been helping support her brother and sister via M-PESA remittances as well.

[Excerpt from *Cash In, Cash Out Kenya: The Role of M-PESA in the Lives of Low-Income People*, Cohen, Monique and Stuart, Guy, Financial Services Assessment, July 2011]

ACKNOWLEDGEMENTS

This book was made possible by a generous grant from The Rockefeller Foundation, initiated by Wiebe Boer in 2010 when he was director of the Foundation's office in Nairobi, Kenya. The primary mandate was to write a "journalistic, narrative-driven story" about the birth and development of M-PESA, and to chart its "seismic impact on the lives of ordinary Kenyan people." A secondary mandate was to show how "the ubiquity of mobile allows the potential for financial innovation in developing countries, especially among those at the base of the pyramid." The grant was to the GSMA Development Fund (the global mobile phone association). Chris Locke, Director of the Development Fund, administered and split the grant between the two authors.

The authors' research and writing was accelerated by matching Bellagio Fellowships from The Rockefeller Foundation, which allowed us to work together for a month at the Foundation's Bellagio Centre (Villa Serbelloni) in Bellagio, Italy, a (quasi) midpoint meeting spot between Nairobi and Boston. Director Pilar Palacia ensured a peaceful environment without interruptions, a perfect environment for writing.

During the initial framing of the book and throughout the writing, we had conversations and interviews with numerous people who were close to the M-PESA story, including (in alphabetical order of the last name):

Kamal Budhabhatti, Founder and CEO of Craft Silicon, an international software company with headquarters in Nairobi, Kenya;

Charlene Chen, Product Manager at KickStart, which manufactures and sells foot-powered water pumps in Africa;

Frederick Eijkman, Co-founder and CEO of Pep Intermedius, which owns and operates numerous M-PESA agencies;

Wolfgang Fengler, Lead Economist in the Nairobi office of the World Bank;

David Ferrand, Director of Financial Sector Deepening in Nairobi;

Jared Getenga, Project Manager, Kenya Credit Information Sharing Initiative;

Nick Hughes, the "godfather" of M-PESA dating to his tenure at Vodafone, and who is now a Director of SignalPoint Partners;

Steve Isaboke, General Manager of MultiChoice Kenya, a satellite TV service;

Michael Joseph, former CEO of Safaricom, who oversaw the deployment and diffusion of M-PESA, and is now Director of Mobile Payments at Vodafone, as well as a Fellow at the World Bank;

Meoli Kashorda, Professor at United States International University (USIU) Kenya and Director at Kenya Education Network (KENET);

John Kieti, Manager at m:Lab East Africa, which is helping to build knowledge companies;

Jay Kimmelman, Co-founder and CEO of Bridge International Academies, a chain of cashless schools in Kenya;

Professor Muragu Kinandu, Professor and Executive Director of the Kenya School of Monetary Studies (KSMS);

Mathew Krueger, formerly in the department of m-banking research and strategy at Equity Bank;

George Maina, former CEO of Musoni in Kenya, a cashless microfinance institution;

Ignacio Mas, former Deputy Director at the Bill & Melinda Gates Foundation, now a mobile money consultant who has published widely on the topic;

Jesse Moore, former Director of the GMSA Development Fund who had initiated talks with The Rockefeller Foundation, and who is now a Director at SignalPoint Partners in Nairobi;

Matu Mugo, Assistant Director of Supervision at the Central Bank of Kenya;

Betty Mwangi, General Manager of Financial Services at Safaricom;

Stephen Mwaura, Head of Payments at the Central Bank of Kenya;

Bitange Ndemo, Permanent Secretary, Ministry of Information and Communications in Kenya;

Njuguna Ndung'u, Governor of the Central Bank of Kenya;

Susie Lonie, who led Vodafone's efforts on the ground in Nairobi during the pilot and launch of M-PESA;

Amollo Ng'weno, Co-founder of Africa Online, then a Deputy Director at the Bill & Melinda Gates Foundation, who is now Managing Director of Digital Divide Data, Kenya;

David Porteous, Founder and Director of Bankable Frontier Associates, and known as one of the pre-eminent global consultants in mobile finance;

Nat Robinson, CEO of Juhudi Kilimo, a microfinance institution in Nairobi, Kenya;

John Staley, Director of Mobile Money at Equity Bank;

Guy Stuart, a Fellow at the Ash Center, Harvard University, who has collected and analysed diaries of M-PESA users;

Professor Timothy Waema at the University of Nairobi, a leading ICT policy researcher and consultant.

Rob Wilkinson, who was Head of Policy and Research at DFID when that institution funded the M-PESA pilot, and is now a faculty member at The Fletcher School (Tufts University).

Kim Wilson, a Lecturer in international business at The Fletcher School, and Director of The Fletcher School Leadership Program in Financial Inclusion.

The user profiles that begin and end many of the chapters were collected by research assistants from the University of Nairobi, led by Sammy Maina and Hellen Kabira, and from Strathmore University, led by John Wachira.

Many thanks to Safaricom, which gave us access to M-PESA agents, partners and customers, and to the GSMA Development Fund, which provided travel and research support. The University of Nairobi gave Tonny Omwansa local logistical support and time off to focus on the book.

Finally, we are grateful to Guardian Books, and acting publisher Katie Roden, who originally published this book in Kindle format; to Edward Peppitt, who ushered the book into print through the BallonView imprint; and to the GSMA's Jody Delichte, who was instrumental in launching the book in Milan, October 2012.

Tonny K. Omwansa & Nicholas P. Sullivan

October 2012